To Ella Mae Fincher, who first gave him roots, then wings

Table of Contents

Foreword

I don't remember what I had for supper the night of April 21, 2006. I don't recall what was on TV in the next room or what the weather was like.

I just remember the phone rang, and it was a miracle I even bothered to answer it. I did not recognize the number that flashed across the caller ID.

"Is this Ed Grisamore of The (Macon) Telegraph?" the man asked.

"Yes, it is," I said, trying to be polite.

"Well, hello, Ed. ... I would like to just *buhlee-stah-baranos-tanoke* and add that to the notion that *suree-fomachino-hand-mylee-willin-fanch-eemed*. Is that what you would say? If so, how many? And, if not, how much?"

The sound coming from the man's mouth was a cross between pig Latin, a lowercase poetry reading by e.e. cummings (without the vowels) and a stick caught in the fan belt of a 1972 Gremlin.

I could have blamed it on a bad connection, but I knew better.

"Ed?"

I paused. "Yes."

"Do you know who this is?"

I had an idea – at least enough to make an educated guess. I have been known to get some pretty strange phone calls as part of my job. I have dealt with accents as thick as a summertime patch of kudzu. I have had my ears bent by folks who need to switch to decaf. I have had men who sounded like women, and women who sounded like men.

But I took a chance on this one.

"Hello ... uh, Durwood."

We had not spoken in years, although we had stayed in touch through our mutual friend, the Rev. Joe McDaniel, who introduced us in June 1997.

That was the first time I wrote about the man they call "Mr. Doubletalk." He was one of the most fascinating individuals I had ever interviewed. He had grown up in the Payne City mill village in Macon, taught high school for 10 years, invented something called "Toe Floss" (for people who stick their foot in their mouth) and built a long and prosperous career as a public speaker.

I have known only one other person in my life named Durwood, and nobody ever called him that. They knew him as Muley.

I had never met anyone *like* Durwood.

There was much more to him than the 2,386 words I was allotted to tell his story in my newspaper column. I wrote five books over the next nine years, but the idea of approaching him about collaborating on a book project took some time to come together – for both of us.

Durwood had spoken earlier that day at a function at the Georgia Music Hall of Fame. After the program he headed over to Cotton Avenue to one of Macon's legendary eating establishments, a hole-in-the-wall hot dog restaurant known as Nu-Way. (Nu-Way could be considered guilty of doubletalk. The word "weiners" has been misspelled intentionally on the marquee since 1937.)

When Durwood sat down at the only open booth, he noticed a copy of The Telegraph from that morning. It was turned to my column, as if it were waiting for him.

I had written about a 12-year-old boy. He was a sweet kid, and his family was convinced he was born to be a preacher. But he was having some mysterious health problems. The doctors were baffled. His mother was trying to get him an appointment at the Mayo Clinic.

To help the family with some of its medical bills, a pancake breakfast was being held the next day at Bellevue Baptist Church.

That got Durwood's attention. Bellevue had been his home church. It was where he was baptized. For 13 years, he never missed a day of Sunday School.

Writing a newspaper column is an extraordinary way to connect people. Sometimes it brings people together. Sometimes it brings people back together.

Over the next several months, Durwood became more than just someone I had written about nine years earlier. In many ways we became kindred spirits, traveling in parallel universes.

In February 2007, I asked him to come to The Telegraph. We had dinner with my editor and publisher. The next morning, Durwood "interviewed" several unsuspecting employees on camera. Everyone was told he was an "on-line" consultant from Washington, D.C. They had been chosen to participate in a corporate video.

He doubletalked them left and right, up and down. They never knew what hit them.

Later that morning, I went with Durwood and a local cable television crew to videotape a documentary in Payne City, the mill village where he grew up. Much of what was filmed that raw winter day was inside the home of 94-year-old Mary Lou Whitlock, who had been a close friend of his mother.

After we finished there, we broke bread at that same Nu-Way on Cotton Avenue. OK, it wasn't really bread. It was a hot dog. And Durwood didn't eat any bread because he recently had been diagnosed as gluten-intolerant. But that's another story.

I knew the basic outline of Durwood's life before that day, but getting to spend so much quality time with him made his story come alive in new and different ways.

I took a bite of my hot dog, smothered with mustard and onions, and leaned across the table.

"You have led an incredible life," I told him. "Have you ever considered writing a book?"

Although he did not answer, I knew he was listening. He had opened his briefcase and was fumbling through the chaotic black hole of loose $20 bills, business cards, prescription medicine, Toe Floss, newspaper clippings, his appointment book and cell phone.

I waited for him to finish and looked him in the eye.

"With your permission, I would be honored to write it," I said.

I could tell he was deeply moved by my request. He still didn't say a word. Through the doublesilence he extended his arm across the table.

A handshake.

And so we began our journey together.

He has told his stories on dozens of trips in his Cadillac Escalade. He has summoned me backstage before big shows, wanting to share the excitement of the moment. He has called late at night from hotel rooms on the West Coast and from the back seat of a limousine in Manhattan.

"You will never believe what just happened," he would say. "This *has* to go in the book."

I have watched him doubletalk waitresses, real-estate agents, security guards, carnival vendors and telemarketers. He even tried to doubletalk the voice coming from his GPS – not exactly a wise move when you're counting on "her" to give you directions.

I have met nearly all his friends – an incredible cast of people I am proud to know and now call my friends, too. I have also become acquainted with all five of his rescue cats – Simba, Kip, Boy, Girl and Tarnation, the pesky one with half an ear.

I have watched him absolutely ignore the clock because, after all, there should be an established time zone for Durwood Standard Time. The man doesn't even wear a watch.

I have seen him lose, misplace and leave behind his briefcase, cell phone, glasses and several pairs of socks. He has been self-diagnosed with ADO – Attention Deficit Optimist. (I told him the earliest case study must have been William Shakespeare, who wrote "Much ADO About Nothing."

We have laughed together, cried together and prayed together. I watched him – gracefully – turn 60 on Aug. 31, 2007.

We once saw the sun slip behind the Great Smoky Mountains on a gorgeous autumn afternoon in Knoxville, Tenn. We sat beneath a canopy of a million stars – on an island five miles out in the Gulf of Mexico – and wondered how anyone could look up at that same sky and not believe there is a God.

I have witnessed his tender spirit as he visited my mother-in-law, shortly after the hospice nurse left the cottage behind our home. He made her laugh and brightened her day. And there he was a few weeks later on "The Today Show," making millions of people laugh from Bangor to Burbank.

From the beginning, I made it clear this was his story. As with most biographies, there would be some places he might choose not to go. This does not have to be a confessional, I reminded him.

I have been amazed at his candor. For all his success and the sum of his experiences, he understands he is still a flawed individual, like the rest of us, with human frailties.

He has become part of my family. We have shared some wonderful times together over these past two years.

My wife, Delinda, and mother, Charlie, adore him. My three sons, Ed, Grant and Jake, all look up to him. Durwood has never married, never been a father himself. So, on Father's Day 2008, we asked him to be our children's godfather.

I will never forget the Christmas we spent with him in 2007. He attended church with us on Christmas Eve and stayed for dinner.

At the table I read aloud from "A Christmas Memory" by Truman Capote. It is a favorite for both of us. I read a passage Durwood had mentioned the first time I met him in 1997. His favorite part of the book was when young Buddy and his older cousin set off through the woods in search of the perfect Christmas tree.

"It should be," she tells him, "twice as tall as a boy. So a boy can't steal the star."

They find their tree, bring it down with 30 hatchet strokes and drag it through the woods back to the red clay road.

A woman in a car sees them on the road and stops. She is the wife of the rich mill owner.

"Giveya twobits cash for that ol' tree," she tells them.

The cousin shakes her head. The tree is not for sale.

"We wouldn't take a dollar," she says.

"A dollar, my foot," says the mill owner's wife. "Fifty cents. That's my last offer. Goodness, woman, you can get another one."

And the cousin replies: "I doubt it. There's never two of anything."

No, there's never two of anything. I had tried to think of something to get Durwood for Christmas that year. But what do you get for someone wealthy enough to afford just about anything?

So I drove to the large antique mall inside the building that once served as the mill at Payne City. His mother had worked at the mill. So had the families of his friends.

Inside, I found several old wooden spindles from the mill. One still had strands of cotton on it. It was largely symbolic, but I knew it would have deep meaning to him.

Then I walked to the railroad tracks near the village and found an old rail pin on the ground. As a boy who wanted nothing more than to get out of that mill village, Durwood used to wonder if those tracks would ever lead him out of there.

Now, they bring him back.

I also gave him a small plaque that reads: "The Journey is the Reward."

I have told Durwood many times during this book project to enjoy the journey. He should appreciate the mile markers along the way, pausing to reflect on a life well-lived.

Enjoy the journey.

Together, we have.

– **Ed Grisamore**
November 2008

Homecoming 2008: Durwood Fincher outside his boyhood home in the mill village of Payne City. (Photo by Ed Grisamore.)

Look out world! Durwood was born Aug. 31, 1947 in Macon, Ga.
(Photo courtesy of Durwood Fincher.)

It takes a mill village

Everybody has a first chapter. A genesis. A spring from which the water started to flow.

For Durwood Fincher, it was the mill village.

It is where he said his first words, stole his first kiss and pulled his first catfish from a watery hole at the edge of his universe.

It is where his imagination leaped from the porch after the sun went down, his footsteps racing through the alleys and dirt streets in a game of kick-the-can. It is where he sat and "watched the radio."

The village raised him, nurtured him and loved him.

It is where he wrote, directed and starred in his first theater productions. He would drape bed sheets across the door of his mother's pantry. His playbill took its place among the soup cans and Capitola flour on the shelves behind him.

It provided the first stage he ever stood on.

There have been thousands since.

He grew up in the long shadows of the cotton mill, where the rhythm of life was measured by the giant machines that spit white dust into the air. Being called a lint head was cruel when it was delivered as a jab from the outside world. But it was a term of endearment among his peers in the village. He never saw it as derogatory. It wouldn't have mattered anyway. He had no choice.

He learned life's lessons along the grid of narrow streets – Brigham, Davis, Rose, Green, Comer and Gardner. The houses stood like rows of dominoes. They were stacked so close together you could hear your neighbors kicking back the sheets on a sticky summer night.

The sons and daughters of mill workers had no special privileges, no rank or social status. Their parents had little or no education, unless you counted apron strings and shade-tree mechanics.

But they weren't poor.

They just didn't have much money.

Payne City was a tiny island unto itself, surrounded on all sides by the encroaching city limits of Macon, Ga. It had its own boundaries, defined by geography and economics. The railroad tracks ran north of the village. The lake and creosote plant flanked the border to the east.

And there was Booger Bottom, where the briar patches provided a fortress and the kudzu covered the ditches like a thick blanket. You were warned if you didn't come home before dark, the Mullyhugger would grab you by the ankles and never let you go.

Durwood allowed himself to dream, his head on the pillow and his ear to the open window. He could hear the sounds of train whistles in the night. He wondered if those tracks, just a slingshot from the mill, would ever lead him out of captivity.

The mill frightened him. He saw what it did to people.

"You should be grateful for it," his mother would tell him. "What would we do if we didn't have it?"

Still, he knew there was something beyond the hardscrabble life of a home with no father. His mother would return from her shift, her fingers so calloused and worn she had no fingerprints. The mill had its way of robbing years and stunting growth.

She suffered from varicose veins after standing on her feet day after day. Unlike the men, who could hide those hideous purple-streaked legs behind a pair of overalls, a woman was marked for life.

But Ella Mae Fincher was no different from anyone else who toiled at a spinning frame so that one day their children wouldn't be sentenced to the same existence.

They would come home so tired their fingers wouldn't move. But they would still find strength to fry okra in big iron skillets and change their babies' diapers in the moonlight before the next mill whistle summoned them again.

Durwood would write plays for the neighborhood children and perform them on stage at the village auditorium. He always got the lead role.

"All my life I have been looking for an audience," he said.

His grandmother would pull him close to her bosom and tell him: "If you don't stand for something, you'll fall for anything."

And his grandfather would come behind her, his strong hands pressed against the small of the young boy's back.

"But remember, Durwood. Once you step in elephant manure, you're in the circus forever."

He recalls the first time he saw the ocean.

Ella Mae had taken him and his brother, Roy, to Jacksonville Beach. They stood at the edge, rubbing their eyes in the salt air.

"Look at all that water," said Roy.

"And that," said Durwood, "is just the top."

He never missed Sunday School in 13 years. He saluted the flag every morning as a patrol boy at school.

He loved and was loved.

"The village was full of the kind of wonderful people and rich characters that make you who you are," he said. "I loved them. But I grew up wanting to get out of there, to break that cycle. To me, the village was just rows and rows of houses, little square pieces of real estate where people were born, lived and died.

"I knew I was destined to do something. I hadn't figured out what it was or how I was going to do it. But I couldn't think of anything bigger in my life than to find a way out of there."

And so he left. He shook the dust from his Buster Browns, the ones his mama bought him at Sears, and promised himself never to look back.

But he did.

He has found audiences on stages and banquet halls from Phoenix to Boston. He lives out of a suitcase and works out of a briefcase. He is on the road so much he laughs that he has to check the back of a milk carton to see if he is missing.

There are days when he makes more money than his mother did in all those years of working in the mill. He had never flown in an airplane until he was 27 years old. He has now piled up so many sky miles he has flown around the world the equivalent of almost 200 times.

He has made more than two dozen appearances on national television. He gets recognized in airports and asked for his autograph in restaurants.

He lives in a 14th-floor luxury condominium overlooking Piedmont Park in Atlanta. It's a long way from Davis Street in the village, where on winter nights you had to brave the bitter cold to reach the bathroom door off the back porch.

The mill and its way of life went away. The smoke and steam no longer seep from the red brick. The whistle does not blow or the shifts change.

The village is gone, too. The houses are there, but those who lived and worked in the mill have died or moved away. The dynamics and demographics have changed.

Still, something pulls him back. It is something that defines him, makes him remember and appreciate. He has not forgotten those roots. They still run deep. They grip the earth. They have kept him standing upright.

"It's the journey that's important, not the destination," he said. "If you don't get it while you're going there, you're going to miss it."

Durwood, center, gets ready to board the Bibb Manufacturing bus at the village. (Photo courtesy of Jeannine Morrow.)

Durwood's parents: Ella Mae and Jack Fincher.
(Photo courtesy of Durwood Fincher.)

An angel named Ella Mae

It was always Mae Day in the village.

There was Ella Mae, Beula Mae and Essie Mae.

"I grew up thinking every woman was named Mae," said Durwood.

There was, however, only one Ella Mae Fincher. And she was an angel sent special delivery.

She loved her family. She loved her Lord. She drank every drop from the cup of life.

"Ella Mae was one of the grandest women ever born," said Willene Caldwell Viglione.

"I didn't know anybody who didn't love my mother," said Durwood. "She never had a run-in with anybody, and her door was always unlocked. If someone needed her, she was there for them. It didn't matter if it was five o'clock in the morning or eleven o'clock at night."

If the mill had a matriarch, it was Ella Mae. She worked there for 35 years. When the mill executives decided they needed a "homegrown" social director who lived in the village, they knocked on her door.

She was a large woman, with thin hair, and a smile rarely left her face. She had beautiful penmanship. The words flowed, even though it seemed as if her hand never touched the page.

She was pleasant, personable, smart and funny. She didn't have a mean bone beneath the buttons on her flower-print dresses.

Ella Mae was as honest as the day was long. If she ever did tell a cotton-white lie, it was only about her age. She was always one year older than what she told everybody.

It never mattered, because every day was a gift. She was a living, breathing miracle.

Her parents, J. T. and Ella Jane Tomlinson, never gave up on having a child. The five Tomlinson babies before her were all stillborn. She was their last hope.

Her family lived near the lumber yard close to the village, and her father had a vegetable truck. When he died, she had to quit school and go to work in the mill.

One night she went to a dance at the mill's social hall. Across the floor, her eyes found a young man. His name was Roy Eugene Fincher but everybody called him "Jack."

"He was tall and good looking, with black, curly hair and dark eyes," said Willene. "He had a short neck that made his head look like it was right on top of his shoulders."

Roy asked Ella Mae to dance. He walked her home. They fell in love and were married at the scout hut in the village.

They named their first child Roy Jr., and he was just like his daddy, a chip off the old block. Some folks called him "Catfish."

They were cut from the same coarse cloth.

When World War II came, Jack joined the Army. Ella Mae ran through the dirt streets to meet him when he returned from the war, but Jack Fincher could barely walk. His feet had suffered severe frostbite in the Battle of the Bulge.

He eventually left the mill and took a job as a truck driver. He was gone a lot.

They named their second child Durwood Tomlinson Fincher. He arrived in the world at 2:06 a.m. on the last day of August in 1947.

Ella Mae chose the unique name Durwood, which means "keeper of the door," after a man who was paymaster at the mill. Tomlinson was her maiden name.

"I used to hate the name Durwood," he said. "It was complicated and long. It never fit on any forms. A lot of the other children in the village just called me Dur."

While Roy Jr. took after his dad, Durwood was more like his mother.

"He is the spitting image of her," said Willene. "Funny. Easygoing. Likeable. She was always teaching him and everything she knew, he knew. She would correct the way he spoke, his diction and elocution.

"He talks with his hands, just like she did. He is disorganized, just like she was. I swear you could go in their house and there would be 15 things on the bed. But she was happy, and she made her family happy."

Behind the wheel of his truck, Jack Fincher would be gone for days, sometimes weeks, at a time. In the summers, when school was out, he would let young Durwood go with him.

"My dad was a modern-day cowboy," said Durwood. "I had never been anywhere before. It was a fascinating way to see America. It was the most magnificent thing I had ever done. We traveled all over, delivering supplies. He had a sleeper in the back of his truck, and I would crawl back there and take naps with the wind blowing on me. It was heaven. We would stay at truck stops. We would sleep in rooms with other people. It was a trucker's existence. We would eat at truck stop diners and have things like tomatoes for breakfast."

His paternal grandparents, Joe Herman and Lily Lois Fincher, lived in the one-blinking-light town of Molena, in Pike County Ga., and Durwood traveled there with his family for Thanksgiving. He recalls the town's name, Molena, had struck him as amusing.

So he made a crude joke about it at the supper table. Timing is everything, he later would appreciate. That was neither the time nor the place.

He does remember making his daddy laugh so hard that Jack Fincher almost broke a rib. They were on the porch at his grandmother's house. It was after dinner, the noonday meal in the South, and his grandmother had carefully placed a sheet over all the leftover food to keep the flies away. Everybody was getting ready for a slice of caramel cake for dessert.

The porch was a place to swap stories, so Durwood repeated a joke he had heard about two little boys.

"My instincts tell me I am going to be rich and famous one day," said the first little boy.

"My end stinks, too," said his friend. "But it don't tell me nothing!"

He can still hear his father's laughter shaking the planks on the big porch.

"I thought to myself, I can bring the house down if I find the right time," he said.

Ella Mae worked in the spinning department at the mill, where the frames would twist the cotton fibers into yarn. It was backbreaking labor. The lines on her face were like rings around a tree. The job aged her. But she always managed to find time for her children.

Her husband, however, was a different story. He would come home with the demons riding shotgun. She would not let him into the house with alcohol on his breath, and one day she had to beat the tar out of him with a belt. She could not take the drinking. So she sent Jack Fincher away. Durwood was 8 years old.

"I asked her why my father didn't live with us anymore," said Durwood. "She still loved him, but she had made a vow not to raise her two boys in that environment."

She kept thinking he would change, hoping he would change. But he would always go back to the bottle.

At night, after she put her children to bed, the tears would fall at Ella Mae's feet. Divorced women were frowned upon in society. People would whisper and point.

But she had no choice. In making that decision, she taught her sons a valuable Christian lesson.

"She told us never to hate him," Durwood said.

If the doors at Bellevue Baptist Church were open, Ella Mae and her boys were there. If the school bells were ringing, Roy and Durwood were sitting at their desks.

"When we would go somewhere, I would always attend Sunday School at another church so I could keep my perfect attendance record going," he said. "It was important to me."

In 12 years of school, he only missed three days.

"The way I looked at it, that only gave me Saturdays to get sick," he said, laughing.

The mill provided a bus to the church. Attending worship service wasn't required, but it was expected. It was a way of life in the South in the 1950s.

"I thought it was odd when people didn't go to Sunday School and church," said Durwood. "I think I loved it because of the socialization. I was comfortable there. Mama had to make Roy go. But I loved it."

Every Sunday, she would press two quarters into his hand and give him a small white envelope to fill out. He would write his name and check off the little boxes.

He would put his money into the envelope. It was a large amount for a 10-year-old boy in 1957. It would buy a lot of comic books and hard candy.

"Why am I giving 50 cents?" he would ask Ella Mae. "I'm not making any money. I shouldn't have to tithe."

Ella Mae would give him a firm, but loving, look.

"One day you will know why you did," she said.

Durwood, right, and Pearl Whitlock enjoy a ride in their "homemade" wagon. (Photo courtesy of Pearl Whitlock.)

The good things never wash off

There were times when her friends and family thought Ella Mae might remarry, but she never did. She raised her sons alone in a six-room house on Comer Terrace. It was divided into a duplex, and they shared a bathroom with the family next door.

Ella Mae had a great deal of pride in the way her children looked. The sons of other mill workers wore overalls to school, but not Roy and Durwood.

"I don't want you to have to apologize for anything," she would tell them.

The stigma of being a single parent wasn't as pronounced in the village. It was like one big family. Everybody not only knew everybody's name, they knew the names of their dogs, too.

Maybe that's what William Sims Payne had in mind when he quit his furniture business and opened a cotton mill in 1899. Six years later, he sold the mill to Bibb Manufacturing Company, but the name carried on. Soon the 14-acre village carried the Payne name, too.

The first houses were built along Green, Davis and Brigham streets. Rose Street got its name because it was lined with rose bushes. Picking them – or any other flower in the village – was prohibited. The speed limit on each of the streets was 8 m.p.h., although it was raised to 15 m.p.h. when the world started moving a little faster.

The village provided almost everything. There was a town marshal, doctor and social director. There was a men's club and a women's club. There was an auditorium, clubhouse, community garden and one of Macon's first neighborhood swimming pools. The village held its own church services on Sunday, and the youngsters had parks, playgrounds and sandlot baseball fields. The boys had their own Cub Scout and Boy Scout troops. Young women participated in the Girl Reserves Club, which was organized through the YWCA.

There was a strong commitment to family life. Trips, banquets, parties and day camps were planned for the mill employees and their families.

"I didn't have any kinfolk, but I was related to everybody," said Durwood. "If you did something you weren't supposed to do, your mother knew about it before you got home. You didn't have just one mother. You had a lot of mothers."

Mavis Horton was one of those "mothers." She was close to Ella Mae because her husband, Emmett, and Jack Fincher had enlisted in the Army at the same time and were stationed at Camp Blanding near Starke, Fla.

"Everybody helped everybody else," she said. "When our husbands were in the service, we would gather at my house to visit and share. The village was the most wonderful place to raise a family. You didn't really worry about your children. Somebody was always looking out for them."

Durwood spent a lot of time in the home of his Aunt Mabel Lee. She wasn't really his aunt. She was just a friendly neighbor.

"I was 35 years old before I realized she wasn't my aunt and Uncle Milton wasn't my uncle," he said, laughing.

Another woman was called Granny. They were not related by blood, only by the bond of the village.

"She lived in this shack of a house and collected what-nots. Everybody gave her stuff," he said.

One day, some of those what-nots got broken. A tornado swept through the village. Trees were blown down, including a huge oak in Granny's yard.

"We had no warning," said Durwood. "We were all scared and huddled around Granny. That was one of the first times in my life I think I experienced gratitude. After looking around and seeing all the damage, I was grateful to be alive. We had all gone through this terrifying experience. But we had survived it, and that was what was important.''

For Durwood, it was a time to grow, his mind fertilized by a village rich in colorful personalities and old-fashioned values.

"They were larger-than-life characters who lived in tiny houses," he said. "They stood their ground. And I observed the way they lived. I am a composite of growing up in that wonderful environment where people knew you and cared about you."

Durwood played beneath the sugarberry trees, planted scuppernongs next to his back porch and fed every stray cat in the village. He drove his neighbor, Floy Parker, crazy while learning the violin. They lived in the same duplex. He would practice while she and her husband were trying to sleep after their night shifts. They could hear him draw back the bow against the strings on the other side of the wall.

"He could be the most aggravating young 'un, and also the sweetest," said Joyce Pyrz, who moved into the Finchers' house on Comer Terrace after they moved two blocks over to Davis Street. "He was always into something."

He spent countless hours trying to catch "Wilfred," the legendary bass who eluded everyone who wet a hook at the lake down at Freedom Park.

Alice Minton taught him how to fish. She was as bow-legged as a cricket on the end of a hook, but that woman sure could fish. Durwood would dig up worms in his yard and head for the lake with a cane pole. There could be four dozen people sitting on the banks, hoping to catch some bream, as well as a breeze, and Alice would be the only one catching anything.

He was close to his older brother, Roy, yet so far away. Roy was seven years older, so the chasm was deep and wide. His brother was also bigger, faster and tougher.

"He won all the fights," said Durwood. "We would say all kinds of things to each other, but don't you dare say anything bad about me to him or him to me. Our love for each other was deep."

If Durwood's goal in life was to drive his brother crazy, he succeeded on almost every level. When he was younger, he and Roy had to share the same bed. Durwood would gather all his stuffed animals and put them under the covers with him, leaving no room for Roy.

As he grew, so did his imagination. He would listen to the storytellers who sat on their front porches every evening and told tales about hunting squirrels, crooked politicians and being baptized in muddy creeks.

Stevie Pope's family got the first television in the village. The neighbors paraded through their living room just to see it. The Popes probably could have paid for it by charging admission at the front door. There was just one channel, and the programming only ran at certain times of the day. But folks were so fascinated, they would go over just to watch the test pattern.

Before television, Durwood and his friends would sit around and "watch the radio." Conway Whitlock had the first radio in the village. It was an old RCA, with buttons, tubes and scratchy reception. They would sit cross-legged on the floor, listening to the radio dramas of the day – "The Lone Ranger," "Gunsmoke" and "The Shadow."

"You would hear all these different sound effects," Durwood said. "It was imperative you use your imagination or you would get lost in the script."

When the radio wasn't playing, the children of the village were. Durwood would write his own skits and plays. He would hold auditions, do the casting and schedule the rehearsals. The children were allowed to use the big stage at the village auditorium, which was built in 1920.

It was made of stucco and had red velvet curtains and a seating capacity of about 400 people. If there weren't theater fans in the audience, at least there were oscillating fans in the windows to push the warm air around.

The auditorium was used for club meetings, shows, banquets and other mill-sponsored functions. An old plantation bell was used to announce events. It was a welcome diversion from the familiar sound of the mill whistle.

The village held other fascinations. Across the road was "Booger Bottom." Some of the men in the village would go there to gamble.

The older residents had a song about it.

When you go to Booger Bottom
Put your money in your shoes
Cause the folks in Booger Bottom
Got the Booger Bottom Blues.

No youngster went into those woods never to return, but the threat was always issued by every parent. If you stayed in Booger Bottom past dark, the Mullyhugger would get you. No one really knew what a Mullyhugger was, but nobody wanted to stick around to find out.

Sometimes the children would crawl through the huge storm pipes behind David and Jeannine Morrow's house. The network of tunnels ran along Brookdale Avenue, where the Morrows' house stood across from the village.

At night, safe from the Mullyhugger, the village children would gather for games of hide-and-seek and kick-the-can. The rows of houses provided wonderful places to hide in the alleys and under the wide porches.

They were simple games for innocent times.

"We had to be resourceful," he said. "We didn't have a lot of toys, because our families didn't have a lot of money. We had to improvise and use our imagination."

Kick-the-can was a popular game for obvious reasons. Most everybody had a can. Maxwell House and Chock Full o'Nuts could have been national sponsors. Often, there would be dozens of children running through the streets after dark.

"When we would finish every night, somebody would have to take the can home and bring it back the next day," said Durwood. "It was an awesome responsibility to be keeper of the can."

"We would play all over that village," said Pearl Whitlock. "Nobody would lock their doors, and we would go in and out. We would hide under the houses. Never once did we think about getting bitten by anything or the house falling on top of us."

The yards were mostly dirt, and the children would sometimes come home so covered their mamas had to stick them in the washtub just to make sure they had the right son or daughter.

The mill elders collected the taxes and ran the police and fire departments. The town marshal–or "village man" as he was sometimes known – not only kept the peace but reported those with unkempt yards to the mill superintendent.

His job was to inspect the streets and alleys before retiring at night. There was a two-cell jailhouse in the alley between Green and Davis streets, and violators were held there overnight before being sent to the county jail.

"There was never much trouble or a lot of crime," said Flemon DuBose, who served as the town marshal. "About the worst thing that would happen was someone would have too much to drink. I would just make 'em sleep it off in jail and the next morning go over and let 'em go. I would never even make a record of it. I once made the mistake of putting two of 'em in there at the same time, and they wrecked the jail."

In many ways the village people were separated and segregated from the outside world, even if the fences were only imaginary. They would leave those boundaries only to go to Scott's Grocery to put food in their bellies or to Sunday School to put the fear of God in their hearts.

Durwood remembers one boy named Charlie Field, who would visit them in the village when he played baseball at Morgan Field. He came from an affluent Macon family. His father was a neurosurgeon. They lived in a large home near the country club.

"He was the first person I knew who had a chauffeur to drive him around," Durwood said. "He would come to the village in a Lincoln. Then, when he was finished, the driver would take him home. We would just stand there in awe. It was a prince-and-pauper thing. We weren't jealous. He just lived a lifestyle that was so far removed from us. We were from two different worlds.

"Truth was, he was envious of our sense of community. None of us had much money, but we had each other. There were always so many other children in the village. We had it so good he sometimes hated to leave. He had a big yard and nobody to play with him."

There were no revolving doors in the village, but the children would move from house to house so often they would nearly pull the screen doors off their hinges. Sometimes they just stopped and ate lunch or supper wherever they were. They would be fed, just like family.

"There were so many children right around our age we were more like brothers and sisters," said Jeannine.

Pearl was Durwood's first girlfriend. They were the same age and shared the same dreams.

Her mother, Mary Lou Whitlock, and Ella Mae were the best of friends.

"Pearl was the sister I never had growing up," said Durwood. "I felt this kinship with her."

They would play together in the village from dawn to dusk. For years, Pearl's mother, kept a photograph of the two of them in the bathtub together when they were 3 years old.

The good things, though, never wash off.

Brother Roy, left, and Durwood. (Photo courtesy of Durwood Fincher.)

Planting the seeds

Every morning the big, yellow school bus would arrive to take the village children to Bellevue Elementary.

It was a discipline for Durwood. His mother worked the morning shift so she could be there when he returned in the afternoon. In the mornings he had to get himself ready, eat the breakfast she had prepared for him and arrive at school early for his duties as a safety patrol boy.

It was a job he took great pride in, especially raising and lowering the American flag. He saw it as a sacred ritual.

The discipline spilled over into other areas of his life. In the third grade he developed a mysterious rash and missed three days of school. Those were his only absences from the first grade through his senior year in high school.

Combined with his perfect-attendance record at Sunday School, it set the bar high for his days at Lanier High School. During those five years he received an award for never missing a day and never being tardy.

His attendance mark in Sunday School was broken when his mother took Durwood and Roy to Tybee Island near Savannah one weekend.

"I had told myself one day it would have to stop," Durwood said. "I couldn't grow up to be an old man with a perfect attendance record in Sunday School. The beach was the perfect time to end this obsession. But that Sunday morning, I felt as guilty as sin. I dared not to swim too far out into that ocean."

His first-grade teacher, Juanita Kleckley, was a major influence on his formative years of education. She was a single woman – some would call her an old maid – who devoted her life to teaching. She didn't discriminate against the children from the mill village. In fact, after the second week of school, she had all the desks in her classroom removed. Tables were brought in to create more of a sense of community.

She also unharnessed Durwood's creativity.

"She loosened my strings about being able to express myself," he said. "She believed that, whatever we did artistically, it was never wrong."

When Durwood wasn't learning his reading, writing and arithmetic, he was playing. He loved to play.

But his activity was limited to backyards and playgrounds. He never was involved in organized sports. Jack Childs, who was in charge of the fields at nearby Vine-Ingle Little League, once asked if he would like to help run the concession stand.

"I was in charge of making snow cones," said Durwood. "Mr. Childs would always give them a big pile of ice and a little bit of juice, and I would always give them a lot of juice. So all the kids would come to me. Mr. Childs finally caught on to what I was doing. I sold tons of snow cones for a nickel each. I told him I didn't think we were going to go under by putting a little more juice in there."

When a team from the league advanced to the national tournament, Durwood was asked to accompany the team to Shawnee, Okla., as equipment manager.

"It was one of the most thrilling things I had ever done, and the closest I had ever been to being on a team," he said. "The coach smoked cigars on the bus the whole way out there. I knew then I was never going to be a cigar smoker. I also wanted to get a sign for the bus. I made this silly little sign. I didn't have any money. It was pathetic. When the bus came to pick us up, someone from the newspaper had made a professional sign. It was nice. I was grateful we didn't have to use my stupid sign."

He never received a trophy for playing sports, but his accomplishments off the field made up for it. His mother had gotten him involved in scouting. He was a member of Cub Scout Den 3 and Boy Scout Troop 2, both sponsored by the mill. His scoutmaster was T. J. Cobb, who was related to baseball great Ty Cobb.

Durwood became one of the youngest Eagle Scouts in his troop, earning all 21 merit badges.

"To this day, I still don't know how I passed the physical fitness part of it," he said. "But it meant a lot to earn my Eagle Scout."

Spelling was his favorite subject. He was fascinated with the sounds and formations of words. He remembers watching "The Ed Sullivan Show" one Sunday night. A man who called himself "Professor Backward" made a guest appearance on the show.

His real name was James Edmondson Sr. He practiced a type of "controlled dyslexia." In addition to being a stand-up comedian, his act featured a unique talent. He could read inverted words on a blackboard and write backward and upside down. He also could pronounce words backward.

It marked the beginning of Durwood's lifelong attraction to phonetics.

When he was 11 years old, he and his mother went to the local Church of God. They took a mentally and physically challenged girl from the village with them.

"Her body was as twisted as a pretzel," said Durwood. "She would get frustrated and have to slap to make words. I had never been in that church. Suddenly, a man jumped from behind us and started speaking in tongues.

"The girl just fainted in my arms," he said. "It was shocking. At that moment, the seeds were probably planted for my life in doubletalk."

Durwood enjoys a laugh on the set with Regis Philbin and Don Rickles.
(Photo courtesy ABC-TV.)

By the way, are you watching TV?

Raising her boys in a single-parent home and working her fingers to the bone in the cotton mill was no reason for Ella Mae to throw a pity party.

"There is no such thing as a great excuse," she told her boys. "So don't come to me with one."

They had no car, so they would take the city bus downtown. Durwood would ride the school bus every morning and afternoon. The village had its own church services, but transportation was also provided to Bellevue Baptist.

The mill was located across the railroad tracks from the midtown neighborhoods along Vineville Avenue. Chichester's Pharmacy carried just about everything. The drug store even sold hot dogs.

It was there Durwood stole for the first time. He was 12 years old. It was only a 3-cent pencil. To this day, he doesn't know why he slipped it into his pocket when no one was looking. He never even got it sharpened before guilt made him retrace his steps to the store.

You could have walked to town on his bottom lip.

"I took it back," he said. "The devil was hanging over my head. I don't know why I stole it. My mother had given me the very best training. I guess I wanted to see if I could get away with it. It was an exercise. I was testing the waters."

He returned to the store and placed the pencil back on the shelf. He left an anonymous note explaining to the manager that he had "done a bad thing and brought the pencil back."

Ella Mae recognized her son's attraction to the stage. She would watch him act out his plays from the pantry. If he wasn't outside, she knew he would probably be at the auditorium.

She encouraged him to perform in front of audiences. She was a member of the Payne City Women's Club. At the Christmas party each year, she asked him to read the poem "One Solitary Life."

It wasn't long before another female influence entered his world. Roy began dating a young lady named Katherine Beasley. They met when she was a junior in high school.

She swept Roy off his feet. She didn't quite know what to think about Durwood.

"He was mischievous and always getting into things," she said. "He would drive Roy nuts because Roy had such a dry sense of humor. Durwood was all over the place. You couldn't pin him down on anything. He was always going here and there.

"Roy didn't have a car when we first started dating, so I would get my dad's car and go get Roy. One day I drove down the alley to let him off at the back door. We were just sitting there talking, and Durwood jumped out from between the houses and scared the living fire out of me. I screamed and screamed. I had never been so scared in my life. I told him I was going to get him, and he went running to his mama."

As much as he grew to love Katherine, Durwood could sense she was taking his brother away. They were married at Katherine's home church, Centenary United Methodist, near the campus of Mercer University.

Roy asked his best friend, Frankie Horton, to be his best man. Durwood was given the responsibility of lighting the candles. When the service began, he could not get one of the candles to light.

"I was so nervous," he said. "I kept striking another match. I didn't even think about taking one of the other candles and lighting it that way."

He was more than nervous. It was an extremely emotional day. With Roy gone, suddenly the nest was emptier. He was the man of the house.

Durwood never missed a chance to entertain his new sister-in-law.

"He always made us laugh," Katherine said. "He would have plays. They didn't have much, but he would take what they had and decorate the house, especially at Christmas. He was quite the showman."

Roy worked as both a firefighter and at Inland Container Company. In 1960, he and Katherine had their only child, Kathy. Durwood adored his niece and spent time with her every chance he got.

"He was like my own personal clown," Kathy said. "He was fun. I always seemed to be in the middle of his mischief. I loved Barbie dolls, and he would play with me. He would dress me up. One Christmas, my cousin and I got wigs. He took out my grandmother's scarves and had us stand in front of this old stereo. He would put on an Elvis record. He gave us toy guitars, and our lips were moving. Daddy was a big Elvis fan, so he thought that was funny."

Ella Mae had worked in the mill since she was a teenager. All those years of toiling in the scorching heat and whirring machines ended when she was named social director of the mill village. With her engaging personality, it was the perfect match.

Ella Mae saw so much of herself in Durwood. But she also saw something else. There was the opportunity to break the cycle of poverty that ran through the village.

"She never even wanted me to go inside the mill," he said. "She always thought once you set foot in there you were trapped."

She encouraged him to work hard so he could be the first Fincher to go to college.

At Lanier Junior High, Principal Johnny Jones asked him to work in the front office. He was dependable and a hard worker. A secretary, Doris Hayes, later asked him if he would like to earn extra money doing yard work at her house.

Her neighborhood might as well have been in a foreign country compared to what he was accustomed to in the village.

The streets were wide. The lawns were green. And the pine trees rocked in the wind as his rake gathered the needles that had tumbled to the ground.

"I remember going home and telling my mama about those trees," he said. "She talked about pine trees blowing in the wind being the saddest sound in the world. She said it reminded her of her mother and father's funerals. That lonely sound represented loss to her. It took her to a bad place."

At age 14, Durwood entered the ninth grade at Lanier High School, an all-boys school with an enrollment of 1,600 students. The school was named after Sidney Lanier, a 19th-century Macon native and renowned Georgia poet.

Two of Lanier's most famous poems – "The Marshes of Glynn" and "Song of the Chattahoochee," – have been eloquently memorized over the years by thousands of high school students.

Durwood, however, had a simple rhyme to get him through those times at Lanier High, where the school mascot was the Poets.

Fake it until you make it.

"It was intimidating," he said. "I figured out if you act like you belong, you don't stand out so much. It was the first time in my life when I started hiding the fact I was from the mill village. It's not that I was ashamed, but there was this stigma. I didn't like the idea of being looked down upon as a second-rate citizen from the village."

When classmates would offer Durwood rides to school, he would walk across the railroad tracks to the corner of Vineville. He would simply tell people he lived "off Vineville." Payne City was never mentioned.

His shoes, however, could not cover up the footprints from the village. At Lanier, white jackets and shirts with button-down collars were considered status symbols.

"I had to wear shirts with big, old collars," he said. "I hated those shirts. I might as well have been wearing a sign that said: I AM POOR."

The great equalizer was the ROTC uniforms that were mandatory three times a week. They were hot and itchy, and he loathed the idea of spit-shined shoes. But behind the Eisenhower jackets and pressed slacks, no one could tell the difference between the son of a doctor from Shirley Hills or 100 percent cotton from the village.

Most of the others his age from the village had gone to Dudley Hughes Vocational School. Only a few, like Durwood, followed the mainstream to Lanier.

He tried his best to fit in. A name like Fincher bought him some time. Fincher was a recognizable name in Macon because of

Fincher's Barbecue.

Doug Fincher, whose family had owned and operated the famous barbecue chain since 1935, was a classmate at Lanier. Some people assumed they were from the same family. But they were not related.

"He played football. I took typing," said Durwood. "One Friday during typing class, the teacher came up and wished me luck in the game. It was my first case of mistaken identity. I really didn't know what to say, so I thanked her. Lanier won the game. On Monday she told me how proud she was of the team. I'm sorry I didn't correct her. That went on for the longest time. I fully intended to tell her I wasn't Doug Fincher, but I never straightened out that woman."

There was still another Fincher at the school, Sgt. Roy Fincher. He wasn't related, either, not in any way, shape or form.

"I wasn't the military type," said Durwood. "I was never disrespectful to Sgt. Fincher. I just wasn't a model ROTC student. I couldn't shine my shoes. I think it bothered him since my name badge looked just like his.

"One time he said to me: 'Son, I want you to do me a favor. I want you to either shape up or take off that name badge.' And, of course, nothing changed."

Durwood got to know the janitors and the workers in the school cafeteria because he could relate to them. He joined the Red Cross Club, the Business Club and Demosthenian Society. Folks from the village usually didn't join organizations like the Demosthenian Society.

He found work to help his mother pay the bills. He took a job as a delivery boy at Hickson's Drug Store, on the corner of Hillcrest and Napier Avenue. He worked at Ingleside Florist, delivering long-stem roses, sprays and wreaths all over town.

He even got a summer job in the crime lab at the city jail. "They locked me behind the bars every day," he said. "It was my job to develop the photographs from crime scenes. Some of those pictures were horrid."

Roy had a 1938 Ford. He would sometimes let Durwood drive it if he was careful. His sophomore year, his mother bought their first car. Ella Mae got it from a man who tinkered with automobiles. He sold her a 1956 Chevy for $500. She borrowed the money from a loan shark because they did not have a checking account.

"I used to take it out and ride around looking at the fancy houses in other neighborhoods," he said. "I would just roam and ride and discover."

He was allowed to have the car on Sunday nights. He would pile his friends in the front and back seat and go cruising.

Sometimes they would ride over to an elegant Italian villa near the campus at Wesleyan College. He had never seen a house quite like that. They thought it was haunted.

Eventually, his father helped him buy a car.

"I paid $75 for it," he said. "It barely had a motor."

He would take his niece, Kathy, for rides.

"He would sit me in his lap," she said. "It was a big Chevy Bel Aire. It was turquoise green, and you could see that car coming a mile away. Sometimes he would work the pedals and let me do the steering. As you can imagine, I didn't do a very good job keeping it between the lines."

At the end of every summer, the big event was Durwood's birthday party.

"His birthday was Aug. 31, and we usually didn't have to go back to school until after Labor Day," said Jeannine. "So everybody would go to his house for a party. We would dance and have a good time. After one of his parties, a lot of us piled into the car and went cruising down Cherry Street."

If he wasn't cruising on Cherry, he was taking laps around the village. He would pick up Pearl, and they would travel in slow motion along the narrow streets. The speed limit was 15 m.p.h., but he could never be accused of speeding.

"It was like he was always in a parade," said Pearl. "He was on stage all the time. One time, he just kept driving. He wouldn't tell me where we were going, and we rode all the way to Atlanta to see 'My Fair Lady.' "

Those were interesting days in high school. The boys went to one high school, Lanier. The girls went to Miller. Absence made the heart grow fonder.

"We hung out together, just like we had since we were kids," said Pearl. "We would walk around the lake, play 'Slap, Kiss, Hug' and 'Spin the Bottle.' We used any excuse to get together. We were all feeling our hormones."

Soon, Pearl and Durwood began to separate themselves from the pack.

"To some in the village, an education wasn't all that important," Pearl said. "But the two of us realized for us to move up socially and economically, we would need to go to college."

His junior year, Durwood went to see the high school counselor.

"She was a socialite who was really into the class system, and Lanier was a college preparatory school," said Durwood. "I asked her about my prospects of going to college. She was not very encouraging. She told me not to get my hopes up. She discouraged me from even thinking about going to college. She told me to go back to the mill and help my family. That was the pattern.

"I didn't think I was better than anyone else, but I did have a burning desire to do something different. The mill didn't represent any kind of future for me. I didn't appreciate somebody telling me I couldn't go to college. In hindsight, she probably did me a favor. It made me more determined than ever."

Years later, when Durwood was a guest on Regis Philbin's television show in New York, his mind flashed back to that afternoon in the guidance counselor's office.

"I thought to myself, I wish I could call that lady and ask her: 'By the way, are you watching TV right now?'"

Durwood reflects at the duck pond on the campus of Georgia Southern in Statesboro. (Photo courtesy of Georgia Southern.)

The land of opportunity

Durwood Fincher not only wanted to escape the mill village, but he also wanted to touch the outside world the best way he knew how.

He wanted to be a teacher.

He wanted to stand in front of chalky blackboards and educate young minds. He wanted his own homeroom, his own grade book, and his own familiar chair in the faculty lounge.

But first, he knew he would have to accomplish something no one in his family had ever done. He would have to go to college and earn a degree.

Ella Mae believed there was something noble about teachers and preachers. Although she never had the opportunity to go to college herself, she was an intelligent woman. She was a voracious reader. She knew Latin. She encouraged Durwood in all his academic pursuits.

The biggest obstacle was affording a college education. It took money to pay for tuition, books, housing, food and other living expenses.

So she pinched pennies and had her prayers answered when she learned about a work scholarship program available through the mill. The scholarships weren't well known or well publicized because few in the village were in a position to take advantage of them.

"If you could get into college, they would help pay your way," said Durwood. "You had to pay them back like a student loan."

When he began the process of filling out college applications, he decided against applying to the state's largest school, the University of Georgia in Athens, because it was too big.

The most logical choice was Georgia Southern in Statesboro. It had a reputation for turning out top-notch teachers. At one time, it was known as Georgia Teacher's College.

He had made good grades in school. He wasn't an honor student by any means, but he worked hard. His teachers recognized he had creative gifts far beyond anything they could teach him in the classroom.

He once took a "Kuder" placement test and scored off the chart in music. That was surprising, since he could barely carry a tune in a bucket and had never played a musical instrument.

He had an incredible retention rate, though. He could memorize anything. (He once learned 67 pages of script for a play.)

If he had one shortcoming, it was his ability to perform well on standardized tests. To further compound his worries about going to college, he was sick on the Saturday morning he was scheduled to take the Scholastic Aptitude Test.

"I was sweating. I probably had the flu, but I had to take it that day," he said. "I left a lot of answers blank. When I walked out of there, I had an awful feeling."

He knew he had done poorly, and the anxious days turned into nerve-racking weeks as he waited for his results.

When he received his test scores, he was elated with the first number he saw. Then he noticed there was a second page. He had only scored 657 out of a possible 1600. That wasn't going to get him accepted into many colleges.

"It was a sinking feeling when I realized that was my final score," he said. "I was very upset. That was the ultimate roadblock."

One afternoon he came home from school. Ella Mae met him at the door, holding a letter. It was postmarked from Statesboro. On the envelope was the letterhead from Georgia Southern College.

She did not say a word. His hands trembled, as if he were reaching into a box with a rattlesnake inside.

"You might as well open it," Ella Mae finally said.

"It was earth shattering," he said. "I was holding my breath."

He read the first sentence of the acceptance letter. And then he exhaled.

"I had been accepted. It was one of the most thrilling moments of my life," he said. "I had to ask: Why me? My standardized test scores were poor. I didn't fit the profile.

"But standing there holding that acceptance letter was very emotional. Mama and I both cried. She was so happy. She saw how happy I was that I was going to study to be a teacher. It was fulfilling one of her dreams. I was her last chance to do something to break out of the village. All the hope she had was in me."

It was 126 miles from his doorstep on Davis Street to his dormitory room on the first floor of Sanford Hall. There was no Interstate 16 back in those days. It was just a long, slow trip down U.S. 80, past courthouse squares and small-town Dairy Queens.

When Durwood arrived at freshmen orientation that summer of 1965, one of the first things he did was to call home. Collect.

"Well, what's it like?" Ella Mae asked.

"Oh, Mama," said Durwood. "You're not going to believe this. There's a shower at the end of the hall."

"You mean you don't have to go out on the back porch first?" Ella Mae said, laughing through tears of joy. "You don't have to hold the hose pipe when you get in the shower? And you don't freeze when you come inside?"

"No, Mama," he said.

He was doing it for both of them. Sure, he wanted to go to college. He wanted to be a teacher. But he also knew his mother was living this dream with him from that threshold back in the village.

"I remember thinking, I've got to do whatever it takes to stay here," he said.

He got a job working in the college's administrative offices. Dr. Ralph Tyson was the dean of students. He was an imposing man. Some folks thought he was mean as the devil, that the grass died under his feet when he walked through campus.

But Durwood admired and respected him. One afternoon he summoned the courage to stick his head in the door to ask him a question.

"I've been thinking about this since I got accepted here," he began. "I didn't do well on the SAT. I did get the scholarship through Bibb Manufacturing. But how did I get in?"

Tyson told him the college had looked at his grades, which were generally good. The admissions office recognized his standardized test scores did not match up with his academic potential.

"We have to make exceptions, and you were one of our exceptions," he said. "You had five great letters of recommendation. You really didn't qualify. It was up to the discretion of the school."

Later, Durwood would compare it to someone throwing him a life preserver.

"I hadn't expected a break," he said. "I guess that's why I was so grateful. Somebody had given me a chance, and I needed that chance. There was no Plan B. I often wondered what I would have done. What would my life have been like? I didn't want money. I didn't want fame. I just wanted to be a teacher."

Durwood takes a sip of "Coca-Cola" to celebrate his freshman year at Georgia Southern. (Photo courtesy of Georgia Southern.)

Durwood grins after catching the garter at the wedding of roommate Joe McDaniel and his wife, Cynthia. (Photo courtesy of Joe McDaniel.)

Life 101

He left Payne City the week after his 18th birthday. He had never called any place but the village home. His only two addresses had been Comer Terrace and Davis Street. And you didn't find either of those on any Rand-McNallys.

As excited as he was about this brave, new world, the pain of separation was almost too much to bear.

He was very close to his mother. He could count on one hand the number of times they had not gone to sleep under the same roof.

And now he was leaving her. She would be alone. He was on his own.

"For me, the thing that smoothed the rough part of leaving home was that she was so supportive. She saw this was something that had to be," he said. "She wanted me to be a teacher. It thrilled her to be able to tell people I was going to college."

The day he left, he hugged his mama. They both cried.

He rode to Statesboro with two other students. Ella Mae packed them all a lunch. It was much more than sandwiches, apples and cookies. It was a basket of love.

Coming from a small house in the village, Durwood was excited about moving into a large, men's dormitory. The dorm fascinated him. He spent hours exploring the campus.

There were rules, though. Freshmen couldn't have cars and had to wear "rat" caps. Everyone had to be in the dormitory by 10 p.m. and lights out by 11 p.m. There were bed checks every night.

In many ways this was a chance to make a clean start. The playing field was level. No one knew about those cotton mill roots.

In college the class structure wasn't as obvious as it had been at Lanier. There wasn't a pecking order.

He had a chance to re-invent himself. And he did.

The week of freshman orientation always ended with a talent show at the Hanner Fieldhouse. Durwood not only auditioned for a spot in the show, but he was also chosen as master of ceremonies for the event.

For his talent he played "Somewhere My Love" from Dr. Zhivago. At least he "tried" to play it on the piano. Every fourth note, he intentionally hit the wrong note. He also told jokes as he played.

Being the emcee helped him make a name for himself. Of course, how could anyone forget a name like Durwood Fincher?

He fell in love with Georgia Southern and its stately campus. He worked in Dean Tyson's office. He became vice president of his class. He worked for the school newspaper, The George-Anne.

But nothing topped the time the dormitory held elections. Durwood ran for fire marshal.

He actually had opposition. The student who was running against him stood up and gave a three-minute speech about fire safety.

"I made one promise," Durwood said. "I promised if there ever was a fire I would help put it out."

His motto? *If you smoke, I'll throw your butts in the can.* He could have started with his roommate, who smoked unfiltered cigarettes.

He won in a landslide. After the election, everyone celebrated by going to the Burger Barn for a cheeseburger.

But the carefree 1960s had an edge, especially if you were a young man of draft age. It was the height of the Vietnam War. Although Durwood had four years of ROTC at Lanier High, he did not consider himself a candidate to become a four-star general one day.

The draft loomed. His number was 63.

"It was all chance," he said. "It was not a low number. It was a medium number."

He returned to Macon and left with five busloads of young men. They reported for physicals at the old Ford Motor plant on Ponce de Leon Avenue in Atlanta.

"They herded us through like cattle," he said. "We had to follow yellow lines to all the different stations. I was classified as 4F. I was large and not physically fit, so they did not take me. As I was leaving, I noticed the guy who had sat next to me on the bus was getting sworn in. A lot of people did not come back with us. My mother was so happy I didn't have to go."

Durwood breathed easier, too. He did not relish the thought of life in the military. It terrified him.

"You will be among the first to go ..." his ROTC instructor once screamed in his face, "... after the last pregnant grandmother has gone."

He spent his freshman and sophomore years at Sanford Hall. His junior and senior years he moved to Brannon Hall. It was there he met Joe McDaniel. They only roomed together for two quarters. But it was the beginning of a lifelong friendship.

"We were the original odd couple," said Joe. "He was messy, and I was meticulous. I was a P.E. major, so I enjoyed sports. He was into everything else."

They did have one thing in common, though. They were both from Macon. Joe had attended Willingham High School in South Macon.

Ella Mae adored Joe. She saw him as a fine, Christian young man who came from a solid family. She knew he would have a steady influence on her son and asked him to keep Durwood straight.

"She had the most wonderful Southern accent I had ever heard," Joe said. "She called him 'Duh-wood.' She wanted him to stay on the right path. She told me she would rather have him go to heaven saying his ABC's than to go to hell quoting Shakespeare."

There were many weekends when Georgia Southern was a suitcase college. Whenever Joe would return to Statesboro on Sunday nights, Durwood knew he had brought back more than just his clean clothes.

"My mother would send back snacks and other goodies," Joe said. "Durwood would walk into the room, never say a word and open that big coffee can and start eating cookies."

It showed. He looked like he never missed a meal, and he rarely did.

"He was a big guy," said Joe. "He didn't have cool clothes and nothing seemed to fit him very well. But his personality superseded all those things. Everybody loved to be around him. He could walk in and be the life of the party."

He had a quick wit and could make a joke out of almost anything. He loved Johnny Carson and especially Red Skelton.

Durwood first majored in English. His interests then shifted to speech and drama. Once again it was his fascination with words that romanced him. One of his professors, Dr. Clarence McCord, encouraged his use of phonetics. Durwood fell in love with the English language and its rich sounds. He was so much in love that he had a 99 average, the highest of all his college courses.

"Dr. McCord was this odd little man. He was more like an insurance salesman or someone who sold Britannica Encyclopedias," said Durwood. "He had developed his own style. It was some sort of gibberish. Nobody would have called it doubletalk back then. He would make up these little sounds, and we would have to transcribe them.

"His goal was to get us in tune with our own speech patterns. It really helped me because I had a lazy tongue. There was one teacher who was convinced I shouldn't pursue speech because I had a heavy Southern accent."

Because he was a born entertainer, Durwood loved movies and the theater. He adored Julie Andrews. To him, she was the epitome of a woman. The guys in the dorm soon learned if you wanted to get under Durwood's skin, just say something less-than-virtuous about Julie Andrews.

He may have set a record for going to see "The Sound of Music." But another sound of music also spoke to him. It was the music of Macon native Otis Redding. When Redding was killed in a plane crash in December 1967, he wasn't much older (26) than Durwood.

Durwood, who was home from college for the Christmas holidays, attended Redding's funeral at the Macon City Auditorium. More than 4,500 mourners crowded into the building and more than 25,000 people viewed the body, making it one of the largest funerals in city history.

Singers Little Richard, James Brown and Joe Tex were there. Joe Simon sang "Jesus Keep Me Near the Cross" and Johnny Taylor performed "I'll Be Standing By."

Durwood sat in the balcony, near the edge. He was one of the few whites in attendance. It hadn't been that long since he had been in that same building, underneath one of the largest copper domes in the world. It was where he had walked across the stage to receive his high school diploma.

"I wasn't going to be a gawker," he said. "I just wanted to be there. He was from Macon. I was from Macon. I was a fan. I couldn't believe all the people and all the flowers. I remember them carrying that casket down the steps outside the auditorium, and all the grieving and wailing. There was pushing and shoving and all this mass hysteria. And I remember being horrified that they were going to drop that casket."

His senior year, Joe McDaniel was hired as a coach at Greene County High School. In preparation for his new job as an assistant football coach, he was sent a playbook.

Durwood walked into the room one night and asked Joe what he was doing.

"I'm studying these plays," said Joe.

"Thank God I finally reached you," said Durwood.

Durwood was convinced he had converted his roommate from his jock mentality.

Said Joe: "He thought I was reading Shakespeare."

Ella Mae poses near a bridge on her trip to Panama.
(Photo courtesy of Durwood Fincher.)

Ma Fincher's new home

Ella Mae was a perfect fit in her job as social director. She enriched lives and nurtured the children in Payne City. You could count on her for anything and everything. She was the mill matriarch, the village mother hen.

Then, one day it stopped. Her position was eliminated. She faced a choice of going back to work in the mill or being unemployed.

So Durwood did something he later would look back on as one of the most rewarding things he had ever done.

He was vice-president of the senior class at Georgia Southern. He was popular with his classmates and the administration. One day he dropped by Dean Tyson's office. He did not beg. He did not plead.

All he did was ask for an opportunity to take Ella Mae from the only environment she had ever known. He wanted to sweep her away to a place of higher education, where sweet young co-eds from Fitzgerald and handsome young men from Newnan left their mamas and daddies to learn about life, love and literature.

He asked Dean Tyson if the college would help him find his mama a job.

"It was the only time I asked them for anything," he said. "So I took her down there and said: 'Here she is!' And then I left her with them. I got in my car and drove around. I knew what I wanted to happen. I came back and found out she loved them, and they loved her. It was a done deal. It was like I had won the lottery."

Durwood was graduating, and leaving Georgia Southern for a teaching job in Columbus.

The college was losing one Fincher but gaining another. Ella Mae was hired to be a "dorm mother" for a women's dormitory.

She was scared to death.

"Just act like you know what you're doing," Durwood told her. "Remember, Mama, these are freshmen girls. Don't give yourself away."

She became "Ma Fincher."

Life on a college campus was as much of an adventure for her as it had been for her son four years earlier. Although she never had the opportunity to complete her education, she had a thirst for knowledge. One of her favorite hangouts was the college library.

She was hired to serve as a "house mother" at three different dormitories – Oliff, Sanford and Cone. After one year at the women's dorm, she asked to be moved to a men's dormitory.

She was more comfortable around boys, she told them. After all, she had raised two of them.

When Durwood would drive back to Statesboro to visit her, he was always amazed at how she had fit in. He was grateful to have been able to help her improve her station in life in the shade of the big trees along Sweetheart Circle.

Ella Mae befriended an exchange student from Panama. Ma Fincher took Lilliana under her maternal wing. The young lady was a long way from home. Lilliana became so attached to Ella Mae she invited her to visit her family in Panama.

It wasn't like Ma Fincher had been asked over for some fried chicken and peach cobbler in Swainsboro. Panama was another country in another part of the world. Ella Mae would have to get a passport and immunizations.

And she would have to fly on an airplane. Ella Mae had never gotten close enough to touch an airplane, much less meet a stewardess.

She had never been much of a traveler, except for those occasional trips to the beach. And this was Panama City, Panama, not Panama City, Fla.

She was nervous. Her plane ticket was $280 round trip, and Durwood borrowed the money to buy it for her.

"At the airport I went up to the ticket counter and told them my mama was on this plane, and she had never flown," said Durwood.

"I wanted them to know who they were dealing with – a woman who didn't even get on escalators.

"The lady asked me if I would like to step on the plane and get her settled in her seat. You could do that back in those days. Now, you can't even walk to the gate with them. So, there I was, getting her on this plane to Panama, and I had never flown out of the country myself."

He hugged her.

She hugged him.

"I love you, Mama," he said.

He walked with Roy and Katherine to the concourse to watch the plane take off at one of the busiest airports in the world.

The jet roared down the runway, building speed.

"Lift! Lift!" Roy shouted, trying to talk the plane up into the air.

"Lift! Lift!" he yelled.

"Quit being so dramatic, Roy," said Katherine.

At that moment, the plane began to rise slowly, the air hoisting its wings into flight against the force of gravity.

Soon, it was just a tiny speck in the southern sky.

Ella Mae Fincher, former mill worker and current house mother, was a world traveler. It would be her first and last plane trip.

Durwood and teacher Regina Satlof Block at a charity auction for Hardaway High School in Columbus. (Photo courtesy of Hardaway High School.)

To teach is to learn twice

On Sunday afternoon, June 8, 1969, he was Durwood Fincher, vice-president of the senior class at Georgia Southern.

Then he walked across the stage at graduation and became the first Fincher to wrap his fingers around a sheepskin. He attended a Hawaiian luau graduation party. His car was already packed and loaded for Columbus. He was to begin teaching summer school at Kendrick High School in Columbus the next day.

He would be making the transition from "Durwood" to "Mr. Fincher."

In his heart of hearts, he had spent the best four years of his life preparing for this day. He had been nurtured by great teachers and encouraged by what would become lifelong friends. He had spent three months student teaching at an elementary school on St. Simon's Island.

He was ready to shape young minds.

There was also great trepidation.

It started the moment he looked back and saw Statesboro in his rear-view mirror. His heart was racing by the time he got lost in Buena Vista. It was dark and very late.

A college friend had offered him the use of his family's house while they were away for the summer. It was near Fort Benning. It was big and empty when he pulled up at 2 a.m.

He turned the key and opened the door. He sat on the edge of a bed and cried. It was the loneliest he had ever been in his life.

"I didn't sleep at all that night," he said. "I had to be at school at 7:30."

He had been hired at Kendrick to teach seniors who had failed an

English course required for graduation. For some, it was all that was standing between them and their diplomas. They were an odd mix, coming from the other high schools in the city – Columbus, Jordan, Carver and Hardaway.

"It was a melting pot, with no feeling of anything permanent. They didn't know each other and, in six weeks, they would all be gone," he said. "It was all negative. They didn't want to be there. So it was an early challenge for me. There was no Plan B. I had to make it work. I didn't know if teaching was going to be my career for two years, 10 years or 20 years. I had graduated from college 24 hours earlier, but none of that mattered. In that classroom there was no incubator period. There was no orientation. I just stood up that first day and started teaching."

His students, sitting uninspired in their desks, sensed they had a rookie in their crosshairs. So he decided to be up front with them. He told them they represented the first class he had ever taught.

"I knew I had to let them know they weren't going to pull anything on me. I told them they could not possibly fail my course and not get their high school diplomas if they did one thing – if they tried. If they would always come to class, they would get credit."

So he not only taught them, he began to build relationships. They began to trust in him. One girl even confided she was pregnant.

"That summer at Kendrick was a great training ground for me," he said. "What a way to start teaching. These were seniors who had flunked English and not been allowed to walk across the stage. I was taking over where they failed or where somebody had failed them.

"But it was all an affirmation I was indeed headed in the right direction," he said. "I knew I was bringing something with me they needed and I needed. There was this outrageous curiosity on my part to see if I had the mettle to do it."

That summer he got involved in community theater in Columbus. He auditioned for a part in "The Sound of Music" and was chosen for the cast as a member of the ensemble. It was a chance to work with Charles Jones and his wife, Eleanor. Charles was considered "Mr. Theater" in Columbus.

One of the highlights was being on stage at the historic Springer Opera House, which later would be designated as the "State Theater of Georgia" by Gov. Jimmy Carter. Durwood will remember the show on July 16, 1969, not because of the performance but because of what happened during intermission.

As the cast was stepping on stage, Apollo 11 astronaut Neil Armstrong was on a larger stage, taking "one small step for man" on the surface of the moon.

"We were watching backstage when it landed at intermission," said Durwood. "When the curtain went up for the second act, the entire cast and crew had gathered in a semicircle on the stage. Well, everybody except Captain Von Trapp. He was some actor they had brought in from New York, and he was upset that we had ruined the show. But we were proud. The audience was proud. America had landed on the moon. Together, we all sang the national anthem and there wasn't a dry eye in Muscogee County."

In the fall Durwood began his duties at Hardaway, a public school that drew from some of the city's upper class neighborhoods.

From the beginning, one of his closest friends was a young teacher named Regina Satlof Block. She had started at Hardaway the year before. She taught journalism and was faculty advisor for the award-winning student newspaper, The Hawk Talk.

Durwood taught English and speech and was given the challenge of starting a drama department. He was later given the responsibility of the school's debate team.

Regina and Durwood were a sounding board for one another, and supported each other's efforts.

"We connected because our students were so similar," said Durwood. "They were artistic and creative. She encouraged me and made sure the student newspaper gave me a lot of support."

It was an exciting time for both of them.

"His talent was to attract a lot of students to theater who normally wouldn't be drawn to drama," said Regina. "It was his personality. He got some popular kids, football players and cheerleaders, and introduced them to the theater."

Rebecca "Becca" Fordham Black was one of those cheerleaders who became interested in theater, even though she never made it on stage. Becca became a fixture at Durwood's rehearsals. It would be the beginning of a long friendship.

"He was always making us laugh," she said. "He wasn't your typical teacher. He broke down the student–teacher barrier. People were trying to figure out a way to get into his classes.

"He had this uncanny ability to come in and command the room while, at the same time, being totally aware of what other people needed. He made everybody feel good. He could spot the underdog, the downtrodden. He identified with them. He took the drama department and made it well known. He did the same thing with the debate team. He had the ability to mold, shape and mentor kids."

Durwood became part of their lives outside the classroom, too. If there were rules against fraternizing with students, he largely ignored them.

"He wasn't all that much older than we were, so he was living in that dangerous space where students and teachers look a lot alike," said Allen Levi. "Teachers were not supposed to fraternize with students, but he did. We would go to his house. He was our buddy."

Said Becca: "He was always very careful. There was never anything inappropriate. My mother recognized his brilliance. My father was an ex-Marine who never could understand why Durwood would want to hang out with high school kids."

Despite the exciting things happening in the drama department, it was a turbulent time in the county's public school system. The buses began to roll in from all parts of the city. Court-enforced integration was neither pretty nor easy. There were fights in the hallways.

"Any day at the school was unpredictable," said Allen.

Against that backdrop, Allen took Durwood's debate class as an elective.

"He wasn't a strict disciplinarian, but he was beloved in a way that students wouldn't take advantage of him," Allen said. "He was there to help you, not beat up on you. He didn't have a chip on his shoulder. The classroom was not about him."

Tom Cohen was in the audience when Durwood walked across the stage as emcee of a faculty talent show.

"He went out and said 'Welcome to Hardaway. I'm Durwood Fincher and this is my Shoney's coat ... Home of the Big Boy,' " Tom said. "It was a green plaid coat. I had never seen anybody like him. He stole the show. Kids were running up to the front. People were throwing money on the stage."

His senior year, Tom was named STAR student for Hardaway, Muscogee County and the entire Third Congressional District. He chose Durwood as his STAR teacher. He was on the debate team and had served as Durwood's "teacher's aide."

"He related on a much different plane than most teachers," Tom said. "He was unlike any teacher I had ever seen. He took the desks out of his classroom and put in tables and chairs. You would walk in his room and there were these huge red polka dots on the wall. He had a podium. He taught speech, and I sat in as an observer. He was very unconventional. The students had a lot of input in that class."

There is a traditional saying in theater. If you want to wish someone good luck, you tell them to "break a leg."

Danny Cabaniss actually broke his leg – on the football field – his sophomore year in 1971. As luck would have it, that's what led him to cross paths with Durwood.

"He was the first teacher I ever had who treated me as an intellectual peer," Danny said. "I could talk to him about anything."

It was an odd twist of fate that brought Durwood and Danny together that first year of court-enforced integration. Danny was a good athlete and a promising young running back. The team was going through preseason practices at a time of racial unrest in Columbus. The school board met and decided to postpone the first week of the season until the tension eased.

"The man from the school board was literally on his way to Hardaway to tell our coaches when I broke my leg and tore ligaments in my ankle at practice," Danny said. "That's when I started paying more attention to my academics. I started hanging out with drama and debate kids, and Durwood was their teacher.

"I was dragging around my broken leg with this big cast, and Durwood's room was right across from my study hall. It was always an open class. I was drawn to that room. It was a melting pot of hippies, blacks and Jewish kids. There was intellectual foment going on, kind of a free form and creative way to teach."

Durwood marched to a different drummer on the soundtrack of life. He had the rare gift only the best teachers have. He made students learn without realizing they were learning.

And every day brought another affirmation of his calling to teach.

"I could put my head on that pillow at night and sleep well knowing I had been placed in a position of authority where I could teach young minds," he said.

Durwood sure scored style points with Betty Cabaniss. She appreciated the impact he had on Danny, who was her only child.

"Durwood was like a magnet," she said. "He taught my son there was something in life besides a ball. He had a very big effect on what Danny and many of the others did with the rest of their lives. They worshipped him. He was over at our house all the time. We became his family. He would come over from school and have lunch. One time he brought the entire debate team."

In 1972, Durwood and his drama students presented a play called "The Boyfriend." It was a groundbreaking production for the city of Columbus. It marked the first time an interracial cast had participated in a public school play.

Durwood was excited. History was going to be made. More than 1,000 people filled the theater for opening night. Crews from two of the Columbus television stations were there to film the event.

The first act went smoothly. Before the curtain could go up after intermission, Durwood noticed the TV crews were packing up their equipment.

He approached one of the reporters and asked why they were leaving. The words have never stopped ringing in his ears.

There's no story here.

"They had come looking for a fight," Durwood said. "They heard there was going to be a rumble. But they missed the real story. There were blacks and whites sitting next to each other in the audience. They jumped to their feet when it was over. They were proud. They were crying. And yet it was never documented by the television reporters. They said there wasn't a story."

As faculty advisor for the debate team, Durwood once drove the team to Athens for a forum. They were running late, and he was in a hurry. As he rounded a curve, the door to the van flew open. Rickie Zimmerman, the team's top debater, almost flew out the door.

"Rickie was grabbing on to the door and my life flashed before my eyes," he said. "I thought: This is how my career is going to end. I dropped Rickie Zimmerman out on his head and killed him."

But Rickie held on, and so did Durwood.

While his drama students were getting ready to go on a field trip, something happened that would profoundly shape the rest of his life.

He met Eloise Hope.

And he's still not sure what she said.

Eloise Hope with her great-granddaughters Bates and Anna Pearce.
(Photo courtesy of Jim Gates and Eloise Hope.)

The godmother of doubletalk

As far back as she can remember, Eloise Hope was having fun with words.

She would put them in the blender of life and flip the switch.

Trying to follow her conversations was like keeping up with one of those quick-lipped disclaimers at the end of commercials. Or like trying to read a Scrabble board on a tilt-a-whirl.

She never had any formal training. She called it "doubletalk" for lack of a better word.

"I never really practiced it, and I could never teach it to anybody," she said. "I really considered it a God-given talent."

But what exactly was it? The dictionary defines "doubletalk" as "speech that is purposely incoherent but made to seem serious by mixing in normal words and intonations."

"The secret is mixing up all the syllables, but you've also got to make enough sense so people can understand part of what you're saying," she said.

She would amuse and baffle her friends and family. When she went to college at Auburn, she packed her bag of talking points and took it with her.

The first time she used it in front of a group was during a freshman hygiene class. When the teacher called on her to answer a question, another student sitting next to her dared her to doubletalk. Eloise stood up and took the dare. "Thank you," said the teacher. And Eloise sat down.

At the dormitory meetings at the beginning of the year, Eloise often was recruited to "address" the incoming freshmen about the rules and regulations at the residence hall. Even the flies on the wall were reeling from a bout of vertigo while eavesdropping on those meetings.

Later, she would doubletalk unsuspecting victims at dinner parties and conventions she would attend with her husband. Soon, she was being asked to speak to school, civic and church groups. She was always introduced by another name and another title.

She became the affable imposter. She might be Charlene McGill from the treasury department. Or Mary Williams, a noted horticulturist.

Nobody ever bothered doing a background search on her. They accepted her at face value. That's why she befuddled them before they had time to connect the dots.

Once, she was introduced at a PTA program as the school's new German teacher. She spoke to parents while wearing a long black dress with glasses and a black pocket book.

She could almost hear the restless stirring in the audience.

I can't understand a word she is saying. What kind of teacher is she going to be?

"Whenever someone would ask me to speak, I would," Eloise said. "I never thought about charging a fee. It was fun just to see people laugh."

An executive from Callaway Gardens heard her at a local civic club. He later contacted her about a group he had coming in for a convention at the popular resort, located about 30 minutes north of Columbus. They were looking for a banquet speaker. Would she be available?

"I don't know," she said. "That's a little far to drive for a meal."

"Oh, we'll pay you a speaker's fee, plus your accommodations," the man said.

She went. She spoke. She conquered. And, within a few weeks, she had been extended invitations to speak in Nashville, Winston-Salem and Miami Beach.

It never was a way to make a living. But it helped with the milk money and the house payment, especially after she divorced and was a single parent with three children.

Eloise began working for the Columbus Chamber of Commerce

in 1969. The chamber used her at many of its functions.

"The money sure helped," she said. "I never had an agent or anything. It was a way to supplement my job at the chamber. One time the hot water heater went on the blink, and I remember thinking: 'Oh, my goodness! Here is another expense!' And then the next day, I got a call to speak somewhere."

After her youngest child graduated from law school in 1979, Eloise gave up her job at the chamber and went out on her own. The list of speaking engagements grew longer. She spoke to pharmaceutical companies, bankers, hoteliers and automobile dealers. There were some big names along the way: American Express, Johnson & Johnson, Toyota, Rockwell International and NASA.

Every speech was different because every audience had a different personality. She always went in under the cloak of anonymity. When The Atlanta Journal-Constitution featured her in an article, it referred to her as the "speaker with a secret."

She once addressed a group of lawyers. After doing enough doubletalking to give them whiplash, she quipped: "With y'all being lawyers, I thought you would catch on right away to what I was saying."

In all, her speaking routine carried her to 40 states, Canada, Bermuda and Mexico. She once was asked to speak at Auburn, her alma mater, at a retirement dinner for Ralph "Shug" Jordan, the school's legendary football coach.

After her words kept reversing the field like a slippery-legged tailback, she noticed the coach's wife was snickering.

Finally, Shug Jordan leaned over. "Would you please hush, Evelyn," he said. "I'm not sure what she's saying either, but this woman is doing the best she can."

She spoke to a group of sportswriters at an event prior to the Kentucky Derby in Louisville. She pretended to be a horse breeder from Georgia.

Afterward, a writer from Sports Illustrated magazine approached her.

"I knew you were doubletalking," he said, laughing. "I just didn't know if you knew it."

Following a speech in Miami Beach, a man asked if she had ever heard of a well-known comedian named Al Kelly, who once appeared as a doubletalking judge on Candid Camera. At the time, she had not.

"Well, he's my uncle, and he's the first person I ever heard doubletalk," the man said. "He made a career out of it."

It was a nice ride for Eloise Hope, too. She officially "retired" in 2004 at age 80.

She won't allow herself to get rusty, though. Every now and then, she'll have a little fun with someone on the cereal aisle at the grocery store. Or break in a new teller at the bank. She has been asked to do several programs at the retirement community where she lives in Columbus.

Eloise has never forgotten one of her "victims." He was a young teacher at Hardaway High School.

She delivered a flurry of frenetic phonetics in his direction, sending him to the canvas in a pile of consonants and vowels.

By the time he realized what had hit him, she had changed his life.

"with Eloise Hope... you've got a ticket"

Are you looking for someone who will be a hit at your big meeting? Do you need a speaker who will send them home with something to talk about? Then phone for Eloise Hope.

When Eloise appears as your guest speaker, you introduce her as Dr. or Mrs. So and So, an authority in your field. Eloise's "secret" and yours, is that she is an expert at "double talk". The audience sits back expecting a few choice words of advice. You lean back to watch the fun.

As Eloise begins her talk, the audience is impressed. They like someone who knows her business without being stuffy, who sounds and looks good. Just as the people start to relax, Eloise slips in a few words of "double-talk". A few listeners do a double-take, you see some puzzled frowns, a man rubs his ear, another motions to you to fix the mike. By now, Eloise is really in her act. You notice a subtle change in the audience, eyes glint with sudden understanding as a few people catch on. Someone giggles, another chuckles, a man guffaws; then like a giant wave, the room is awash with laughter, as the audience realizes its been taken in by a hilarious hoax. Your guest speaker is an expert all right . . . an expert "double-talk" artist who is the hit of the program.

HOW YOU GET INTO THE ACT . . . When you engage Eloise to speak for your group, she gives a tailor-made speech. With your help, she chooses a subject to fit in with your meeting. She can appear as an educator, sales or economic consultant, lawyer, banker, professional engineer, psychologist, physician, criminologist, horticulturist or any expert of your choice. Eloise actually makes two talks. First, you introduce her as your guest speaker and she "double-talks" her way through a technical speech. Second, you introduce the real Eloise Hope and she shares her bag of hilarious experiences with the audience. Eloise offers you a unique program idea that has fascinated audiences throughout the United States.

Promotional brochure used by Eloise Hope for her speaking engagements. (Courtesy of Eloise Hope.)

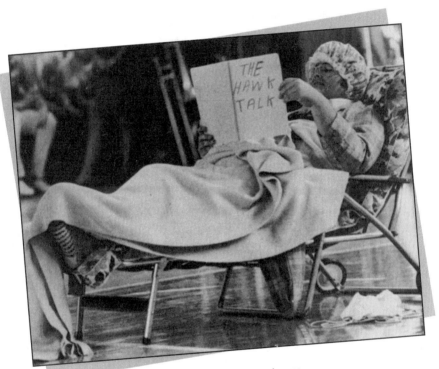

Durwood takes part in a skit for a pep rally at Hardaway.
(Photo courtesy of Hardaway High School.)

Serendipity calls his name

You never really know what a day will bring. You never know if the wind will be in your face or at your back. You never know if a person will show up at your door, either choreographed or by happenstance, and change the pattern of your life forever.

Just ask Joe the Plumber. One day you're fixing a toilet. The next day you're out on the national campaign trail, stumping for a presidential candidate.

Serendipity calls your name.

Durwood scrambled out of bed one morning in the fall of 1971. He didn't have the slightest hint a woman named Eloise Hope was about to provide the divining rod for the verbal trickery that would one day make him famous.

Durwood was taking several students to a one-act play competition. While he was busy loading the cars and getting permission slips signed, the wheels of mischief were turning in Dewey Renfroe's head. Renfroe was the principal at Hardaway and a bit of a practical joker.

Durwood was an easy target. He was a young, conscientious teacher who was rushing around trying to take care of all the last-minute details. The perfect victim.

Renfroe could not resist having a little fun at the rookie's expense. He introduced Durwood to Eloise, who worked in public relations for the Columbus Chamber of Commerce.

Only, he didn't introduce her as Eloise Hope.

"Durwood, this is Mrs. Smith," he said. "She is with the school board. She would like to talk to you about tort insurance for the trip."

Mr. Fincher, I would like to inform you that fir-ee-sum-och-chu-tomoor *and add that to the notion that we* dul-sub-lir-fomak-putch-wetchel. *Would you sign this please?*

"She zapped me," Durwood later recalled. "I didn't feel stupid. I felt vulnerable. The whole conversation didn't last but a few minutes. Dewey laughed until he had tears in his eyes. The kids all loved it because they knew her. I felt so relieved when I found out it had all been a joke. And I could not shake how funny it was and my own reaction to it.

"People tell me all the time I don't know what it feels like to be on the receiving end of doubletalk. But I do. I have been in their shoes."

She never gave him lessons. He learned by observation. He figured out how to string together entire phrases filled with sense and nonsense, jargon and jabberwocky, syllables and silliness.

The students at Hardaway were the mice inside his test laboratory.

"He would go into the hallway, get some unsuspecting student and send them on an errand to the dean of boys," said Allen Levi. "He would doubletalk, and then repeat it three or four times. We couldn't wait to see what the student brought back."

Said Tom Cohen: "He was a novice back then. He had to learn. He had to go out and practice. I watched him develop his skills. It happened in incremental steps. Sometimes he would leave people squirming on a hook, and I was always a little uncomfortable with that. But he was different, talented and special."

Once, when he went home to visit his friends and family, he decided to pull the switch on his fog machine and try out his developing routine.

Gene Morrow's living room was his practice field.

"He was using all these sentences that didn't make any sense," said Jeannine Morrow. "My dad was just looking at him like: 'What in the world are you trying to say?' "

Durwood told him he was thinking about making a career of it.

"Son," said Gene, "I know you're going to go a long way with that line of bull."

It was affirmation from the home front. It was validation from the village.

If nothing else, he had an endorsement from Gene Morrow.

It was true.

Once you step in elephant manure, you're in the circus forever.

He would need to check the bottom of his shoes.

Durwood left teaching for the rigors of a gubernatorial campaign before returning to the classroom. (Photo courtesy of The Westminster Schools.)

Snollygoster meets Camelot

The tiny duplex on 16th Street and the small house on Dinglewood Drive provided the backdrop for some of life's greatest lessons.

"Columbus was the first time I was really on my own," he said. "And it was absolutely frightening. It was almost too much."

A bachelor, he had no one to clean up after and no one to clean up after him. One afternoon, Ella Mae drove over for a visit. Durwood's 10-year-old niece, Kathy, went along for the ride.

"The condition of his apartment and the amount of food in the refrigerator gave no indication he was expecting guests," said Kathy. "We got there after lunch, and both of us were starving. It was a very spartan apartment. He invited us in, and we sat at this little table.

"After a while my grandmother said, 'Well, Duh-wood, have you got anything to eat or do we need to go to a restaurant?' And Durwood went to the refrigerator and brought back one chicken wing and a Diet Sprite and put it on the table. He expected us to share that. Finally, my grandmother stood up and said, 'I am not going to put Kathy through this! We are hungry, and we are going to get something to eat!' And it was OK with Durwood. It didn't seem to bother him one bit."

In many ways, those years in Columbus were among the sweetest times of his life. He was old enough to live in the adult world, but young enough to understand and relate to the youth who filled the desks in front of him.

He was on stage, auditioning for a larger role, and they were his audience.

"I knew I was never going to get rich teaching school, but that wasn't my goal," he said. "I was married to that school. I loved those kids, and they loved me. We got along. There was no question I was on track."

After five years at Hardaway, he was convinced it was time to move on. He applied for a teaching job at a high school in Chapel Hill, N.C. It was a college town. He saw it as a possible springboard to becoming a college professor.

He was offered the job and had already resigned from his teaching position at Hardaway when the superintendent of schools in Chapel Hill called to tell him the position would instead be filled by a minority applicant.

"I was devastated. It was a shattering experience for me," he said. "I became disillusioned about teaching again. I felt I had been handed a deck of cards and they were all jokers. I freaked out. That was one of the hardest things I ever had to take."

At the end of the school year, Durwood had been invited to a pool party for one of his students, Alvin Harris. At the party, he chatted for a few minutes with Alvin's father, a local attorney named Morton Harris.

A few weeks later, Morton got a phone call.

"Morton, this is Durwood Fincher. Do you remember me?"

He told Morton his job in North Carolina had fallen through and he had no real desire to return to teaching in Muscogee County. Surely, a well-connected attorney like himself knew of a job opportunity.

Morton admits he was puzzled by the call. He did not know Durwood very well.

"He probably had called everyone on his list until he got down to me," Morton said, laughing.

Actually, Morton did know of a short-term opportunity for Durwood. He was involved in the gubernatorial campaign for his longtime friend, former Columbus mayor Harry Jackson. It was a crowded field on the Democratic side of the ballot. Jackson was one of a dozen Democrats in the gubernatorial primary.

Morton had some political experience but had no idea what was in store for him. When Jackson's campaign manager suffered a heart attack, Morton had to step into that role. And he was looking for an advance man who could go in ahead of candidate Jackson, setting up press conferences and campaign events.

Rome, Vienna and Athens might sound like a romantic travelogue – except they were all towns in Georgia.

Although Durwood had a limited working knowledge of politics, he was willing to learn. He certainly had the personality for public relations. He viewed it as an incredible opportunity to broaden his horizons.

"Did I think Harry Jackson was going to be elected governor?" Durwood said. "No, I didn't. There were so many other candidates."

There was so much political rhetoric during the campaign that Morton came up with a T-shirt with a caricature of a candidate talking out of both sides of his mouth.

The shirt read: "Help Stomp Out Snollygoster."

Snollygoster was a term first used by President Harry Truman in 1952. By definition, it is any person, especially a politician, who is guided by ambition and greed rather than duty and principles.

Durwood traveled to cities and towns in Georgia he never knew existed. He attended so many banquets and ate so many fried chicken dinners he thought he was going to sprout feathers.

One day he asked Morton if Jackson might attend a political rally in his old mill village. Payne City wasn't exactly a routine stop for stumping on the campaign trail.

"The very idea of getting a candidate for governor to come to Payne City ... well, that kind of thing just didn't happen," said Durwood. "I got Mama to have the ladies to make sandwiches, and we had a little social out there. I think about 40 people showed up. I don't think I've ever been as proud of pulling off anything."

During the campaign he met a man named Joe Phipps who had been hired to produce political ads for the Jackson campaign. It was Durwood's responsibility to take them around the state.

After Jackson dropped out of the race, Phipps returned to Washington, D.C. But he stayed in touch with Durwood. He later contacted him about doing some sound work with his production crew. Durwood traveled to New York, Chicago and Los Angeles to work on a film for the department of energy.

Then time ran out on that job, too. It was the fall. School had started back. He was unemployed. He moved to Atlanta to hunt for a job in advertising.

Milo Hamilton, a former radio announcer for the Atlanta Braves, was doing public relations work for the Georgia legislature at the state capitol. One of his secretaries had worked for the Jackson campaign and knew Durwood.

The office had an opening. It was not a paying job, but Durwood saw it as a chance to get his foot in the door, a springboard to something bigger.

"I had some free time and could type like a son of a gun," he said.

One day, the phone rang.

"Is this the Durwood Fincher who taught at the governor's honors program a few years ago?"

The woman identified herself as a secretary for Dr. Emerson Johnson, the headmaster at Westminster, an elite private school in Atlanta. She said Johnson wanted to talk to him about an interim position at the school through the Christmas holidays.

He was worldly enough to understand the best way to get a job was to act as if he wasn't interested. This time, though, it didn't take much acting on his part. He was genuinely not interested.

Johnson called and asked him to reconsider. He would be replacing a teacher who had been terminated for inappropriate, and rather unusual, behavior. (The man had been smoking cigars in the classroom.)

Although Durwood still played hard to get, he was really in no position to barter. He was flat broke. He was living off crackers and sleeping on the sofa of a friend, Agnes Albright, who lived in a midtown apartment on Juniper Street.

Some nights, he even slept in his car. He had gone to the bank and tried to cash a check.

"Mr. Fincher," said the teller. "There seems to be a problem with insufficient funds."

"That can't be right," Durwood shot back. "I still have a whole pile of checks I haven't used."

He agreed to meet with Johnson. He had to borrow a few dollars to buy gas.

His Toyota Corolla leaned to one side when he was behind the wheel. There was duct tape holding up the exhaust pipe. (The car was silver, so at least it matched.)

There was a marked contrast when he arrived. His clunker was right at home in the faculty parking lot, where there were rows of red Torinos, green Novas and purple Gremlins.

He glanced over at the student parking lot. He lost count of all the BMWs and Mercedes.

The 160-acre campus was pristine. It looked as if had been cut from Ivy League cloth. There wasn't a mill village anywhere in the vicinity.

Durwood turned to Johnson.

"I've got one question," he asked. "Where is Merlin?"

Johnson smiled and took that as a gesture of acceptance.

Said Durwood: "I truly was at Camelot."

Back on the saddle: Durwood rekindled his love for the classroom at Westminster in Atlanta. (Photo courtesy of Durwood Fincher.)

Support your local potter

Being back in the classroom was like riding a bicycle. Durwood's sense of balance and direction had stayed with him.

He was assigned to teach English and speech in the middle school.

"Coming from teaching juniors and seniors in high school, I was going backward," he said. "But I kept telling myself it was only for three weeks."

Or so he thought.

He had gone to Macon for the Christmas holidays. The house was filled with friends and relatives. Emerson Johnson called looking for Durwood.

"He asked if I would finish out the school year," said Durwood. "I hadn't had any problems with the students, and I hadn't been there long enough to get to know the faculty. But I had no other prospects. It was steady work. It was a lot more money than I had been making at Hardaway, and he also offered me a bonus. I could not, in good conscience, turn that down. He was relieved when I accepted. The parents had come after him hard after the teacher had been fired. They were paying all that money for tuition. I had taken the pressure off of him."

Durwood was first assigned to the girls school, then asked to be moved to the boys school. He took on additional responsibilities. He taught speech classes and later theater. For the spring play, he chose "A Member of the Wedding," which had been written by Columbus native Carson McCullers.

"They had been doing all this light, fluffy stuff," he said. "This was serious, heavy drama. It wasn't a musical and had a small cast. We didn't get a lot of exposure."

The crowd was small for the Friday night show, but Johnson was in the audience and was thrilled. So were others. After word got out, there was almost a full house for Saturday's performance.

By the next school year, Durwood had settled back into teaching. Westminster was a nice place to land at this time in his life.

"My passion started coming back for teaching," he said. "I got along with the students, although they came from a different world. Some stayed on campus in the dormitory. There was a lot of pressure on them to excel. I had never been exposed to people with that kind of wealth. It was hard to relate to kids who would tell you they were tired of having to go to Switzerland with their families.

"For me, being around those 'poor' rich kids debunked the myth that having money meant you had it made."

He got along with the faculty, although some were cautious of him. He parked his Corolla in the parking lot every morning. One day, he showed up with a bumper sticker.

Durwood had never been big on bumper stickers. He had never even had one on his car until he came back from a pottery shop one afternoon.

It said: "Support Your Local Potter."

He wasn't a potter himself, but he read between the lines. It was urging support of creative people in the arts. Another faculty member had her own interpretation. She complained Durwood's bumper sticker had a subliminal, subversive message about smoking marijuana.

Durwood was asked to remove the bumper sticker, but he held his ground.

"I will not because I am not guilty," he said.

It was never mentioned again. Years later, when time and the elements left it cracked and faded, he scraped it off the back of the Corolla and grinned.

"I told that bumper sticker it had been a good and faithful servant," he said.

Nancie McManus was hired as head of alumni and development at Westminster in 1976. They became instant friends.

"Like Pearl, she is the 'other' sister I never had," said Durwood.

"I had never seen him teach or seen one of his plays, but he absolutely delighted me," she said. "I was a size 2 and smoked four packs a day. My husband was just starting his law practice. I moved fast, thought fast and I was always in your face with personal questions. I just loved Durwood's mind, how quick he was."

Nancie called him "Dodie." (That's what Durwood's niece, Kathy, and her two children – Kristy and Jason – called him when they were little because they could not pronounce Durwood.)

"We were raised with the same sense of values," Nancie said. "We were very comfortable together. We enjoyed each other's company, doing the same things, cruising around town.

"Part of me also thinks that, for Durwood, I was just a particularly good audience."

After living in an apartment his first year in Atlanta, Durwood found a house to rent at 275 West Wieuca Road. It was convenient to the school and had a screened-in porch, a place where he would stretch out in his hammock one night and hatch the idea for one of the greatest novelties of his generation.

The pay at Westminster wasn't the only benefit to teaching there. Unlike Hardaway, where he would be responsible for five or six classes a day, Westminster operated more like a college campus. Sometimes, he wouldn't have to teach his first class until 11 a.m. Another time, he had a three-hour break between classes.

One quarter, he had several free periods in the late morning and early afternoon. There was such flexibility in his schedule he would sometimes drive to the capitol during the winter months when the General Assembly was in session and do volunteer work at his old office.

In January 1979, Durwood noticed in the newspaper one morning that Deng Xiaoping, the famous Chinese revolutionary, was touring the U.S. His first stop was Atlanta. He was scheduled to visit the Ford Motor assembly plant, then a solar energy facility at Georgia Tech.

Deng Xiaoping was to make an appearance at the Omni at noon, which fit right into Durwood's midday break.

"I told myself I was just going to go down there and see him," Durwood said. "I found the corridor at the Omni where he was supposed to arrive. It was cold, and I had on a black trench coat. When I got there with all those curiosity seekers, I realized I was dressed the same way the Georgia Bureau of Investigation (GBI) agents were dressed. My gosh, I looked just like one of them."

He was standing there, not even trying to blend in, when a GBI agent walked up and asked him if "everything was clear."

Stunned, Durwood nodded and fell into position with the other agents. Suddenly, Deng Xiaoping came so close Durwood could smell the moo goo gai pan on his breath.

He got in his car and drove back to Westminster. He never told anyone what happened until later.

"It never occurred to me that I could have gone to jail for what I did," he said. "It was a fascinating day. It made me realize that if you look the part, your chances were good. It helped me later when I would apply for different jobs. I just tried to look like I belonged. I would tell my students that sometimes you just have to fake it until you make it. Look the part until you are the part."

The man who would later become known as "The Great Imposter" already was auditioning.

Durwood's motto: "Look the part until you are the part."
(Photo courtesy of Durwood Fincher.)

Crashing convention parties was fertile training ground, preparing him for a life in doubletalk. (Photo courtesy of Durwood Fincher.)

All I wanted was a little roast beef

Some people read the newspaper for the want ads. Others turn to the comic page or aim their pencils at the crossword puzzle.

There was always one special feature Durwood would search for in The Atlanta Journal-Constitution. He would check the listings to see which conventions were in town.

He would "crash" convention parties. One night he might pose as a tire company executive from Akron. The next night he might pretend to be an insurance salesman from Dubuque. Or a dentist from Fort Worth.

It all started one night when he attended a meeting at the old Marriott Hotel on Courtland Street. The Marriott was a large, downtown hotel capable of hosting several conventions at the same time. After his meeting, he wandered into one of the ballrooms.

"I was amazed that I could walk around and there wasn't a lot of security," he said. "I stuck my head in the door. I had on a coat and tie and looked like everybody else. I got a name badge and just went in."

Of course, the buffet tables were piled high with food. And he happened to be hungry.

"All I wanted was a little roast beef," he said.

It was an automotive convention. Somehow, this sparkplug didn't fit. Durwood couldn't tell the difference between a head gasket and a tail pipe.

"Don't show me what's under the hood," he said. "Show me where the cup holders are!"

But he looked at the spread of food on all those tables. He was either going to get to that cheesecake or die trying.

He felt a hand slap him across the back. He turned around. It was a guy named Fred. Or Cecil. Whatever his name was, he appeared to be important.

Durwood stopped nibbling on the roast beef and swallowed hard.

"Oh, my God," he thought to himself. "I just got caught."

The man was friendly, though. Durwood made up a name and told him he was from Detroit, which seemed to be a pretty safe alibi. He told him he was new in the business and looking forward to meeting others at the convention. When the man lingered, Durwood reached back and found his weapon.

"He had been drinking, so I started doubletalking," Durwood said. "It wasn't that I wanted to lie or steal. I didn't know what to do or say, so it was a lot easier just to make stuff up. He eventually went away and left me alone. I scared him off."

He may have done it the first time to fill his belly, but every time after that was to feed his ego. He enjoyed the challenge.

"It was the thrill of the hunt," he said. "I never took food home, but I also didn't ever want my mother to find out I wasn't eating well."

Although he never got caught, he did have a few close calls. He crashed one convention but forgot to put on a name badge. Someone came up to him who thought he was somebody else. Suddenly, he was surrounded. He did not know any of them, and he wasn't who they thought he was.

"I was able to doubletalk my way out of it," he said. "I wish I had a camera to take a picture of the looks on their faces. But I came dangerously close to getting caught. I was out of place, and it was getting out of hand."

He found himself eating less and talking more. This was fertile training ground, preparing him for a life of doubletalk. He just didn't know it at the time.

"I kept telling myself there was a reason I was doing it," he said. "I've always said most of us are looking for an audience. This was my audience. I was laying the groundwork. I didn't have a plan. I was just doing it because it was in the moment.

"And it wasn't really hurting anybody. I wasn't being deceitful for a reason. I wasn't taking stuff. I was eating very little, although I did love the roast beef.''

The Original Toe Floss came in a box, followed by the famous plastic canister.
(Toe Floss courtesy of Tommy Teaver.)

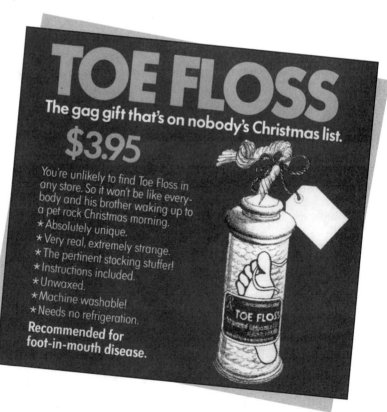

The next pet rock

A typo and a gaffe were his salvation.

It was practically gift-wrapped in a form letter from a theatrical society. He was on their mailing list. When he pulled the envelope from his faculty mailbox, he noticed the label on the address.

FURWOOD DINCHER.

With a name like Durwood Fincher, he was accustomed to botched spellings. But this one moved to the head of the class. He showed it to several friends and other faculty members. It was worth a chuckle.

A few nights later, he found himself at a party. There were several media personalities there, including Atlanta newspaper columnists Lewis Grizzard and Ron Hudspeth. Durwood still had aspirations of getting into advertising. He networked by running in the same circles with folks like Tom Little and Jack Burton. They were giants in the Atlanta advertising world and huge creative influences on Durwood.

"I was standing with a group of people at the party and a comment was made about somebody's sister-in-law," he said. "It wasn't ugly, but the sister-in-law was standing right there. So it was a real gaffe."

Trying to snap the awkwardness of the moment, Durwood decided to add a little levity.

"You need some Toe Floss," he said. "You just stuck your foot in your mouth."

Everyone laughed, even though no one really knew what Toe Floss was. Or what it did.

Of course, it hadn't even been invented. It was still a few hours away from being born.

When he returned home from the party, he retreated to his

hammock on the porch. It was his favorite place to think, unwind and dream big.

Toe Floss. ... Furwood Dincher. ... Foot in your mouth. ... Furwood Dincher. Furwood Denture? ....

As the cars raced by in the darkness along West Wieuca Road, the wheels were turning in his head.

Furwood Dincher's Toe Floss.

It was the kind of chaotic juxtaposing he later admitted "might never have happened in today's age of spell checks."

Two years earlier, a California advertising executive named Gary Dahl had gone to a local builder's supply store, purchased some pebbles imported from the coast of Mexico and launched one of the most incredible marketing fads in history.

He called them "pet rocks." He gave them names. He included a training manual on how to care for each rock and teach it tricks. It sold for $3.95.

Six months later, he was a millionaire.

If someone could sell an ordinary gray rock, Durwood pondered the possibilities of six feet of common rope to help with "foot-in-mouth disease."

He was convinced it was all in the packaging. He just needed someone to help him take this idea, bottle it and market it.

That person was Tommy Teaver.

They met through a mutual friend, Chris Moore. Durwood had taught with Chris at Hardaway. It was Chris who had recommended Durwood for the teaching position at Westminster.

A native of LaGrange, Tommy was working in Atlanta as a typographer and graphic artist. He also was an intellectual giant with a photographic memory. Trying to sneak a trivia question past Tommy was like trying to sneak the dawn past a rooster.

"The first thing I noticed about Durwood was that he couldn't sit still," said Tommy. "He was always wiggling."

Having such a brilliant idea just added motion to the potion. Durwood was like flippers on a pinball machine, the bells ringing and lights flashing in his head. There was no real fear of tilting the machine.

He had everything he needed. A big dream. An ambitious plan. And a friend with brains who was willing to take that leap of faith with him.

There was one problem. Money.

Morton Harris had heard from Durwood a few times since the days of the gubernatorial campaign. He knew Durwood had settled back into teaching and was living in Atlanta. Durwood would sometimes stop by when he came back to Columbus to visit friends.

Morton was relaxing by his pool when the phone rang. It was Durwood.

"He said he had invented something and was coming to show it to me," said Morton. "He was so excited. He got in the car and drove straight to Columbus. He was here in an hour and a half. He showed up with this idea about Toe Floss. All he brought was a design. He hadn't made or built anything. It was just an idea.

"It was pure Durwood, even though it didn't necessarily strike me as the next pet rock. He needed some money to help him get started. I would have helped except I had four children. I didn't have the money. But I knew someone who did."

Jack Schiffman was a wealthy Columbus businessman. In 1950, he was on the ground floor of a chain of women's clothing stores called Casual Corner. Five years later, he loaned some seed money to John Amos who, along with brothers Paul and Bill Amos, started American Family Life Assurance Company, better known as AFLAC.

Durwood once babysat for Jack's children. It was easy money. The Schiffmans already had a cook and a housekeeper. It had been Durwood's first real taste of lifestyles of the rich and famous.

Morton told Jack about the proposal. They met Durwood for dinner.

"I still only had a design, and I could tell from Jack's reaction it was not what he had in mind," said Durwood. "I figured I needed something like $2,800. To me, that was like the national debt. Jack had probably left tips for more than that, so money wasn't a problem.

"I'm convinced he loaned me the money never expecting to see it again. Somebody once told me if you want to make sure people stop borrowing money from you, just loan them a little. They won't go back for seconds. He wrote me a check for $5,000. I thought I had won the lottery."

For Schiffman, it wasn't so much of an investment but an amusement ride.

"I'm going to do this because I think you're just crazy enough to pull it off," he told Durwood. "And it sure is going to be fun watching."

Said Morton: "My guess is he assumed he would never see that money again. But he believed it had at least some potential because of Durwood."

It never was part of a get-rich scheme. Durwood was more excited about having an original idea than the prospects of becoming a millionaire.

He ordered his first batch. The original product came in a box with a rather long-winded instruction manual. Later, he would package it in a six-ounce plastic container manufactured by a company located near the Atlanta airport.

The yarn came from a mill in Alabama. He would drive over and buy big spools of soft rope-like material.

Funny, how he ran so hard from the mill when he was younger. Now, for his first business venture, he was returning to the threads of his roots.

Durwood kept his inventory at his home on West Wieuca. He recruited students from Westminster to help cut, wrap and package each segment of "floss."

"We called it our Toe Floss Factory," he said. "It also taught me that, for the rest of my life, I never wanted to put out a product that either had to be cooked or put together."

Jeff Singer, one of his students at Westminster, was Durwood's one-and-only paid employee at the "factory."

"He would work for hours, wrapping it and boxing it," said Durwood. "A lot of people helped, but he was the one who stuck with me. He was fiercely independent, and he enjoyed working for me."

Life comes with no guarantees. There are garages and storage sheds from Wieuca to Walla Walla full of best-sellers that never sold and inventions that didn't fly.

"Sometimes you have to be willing to make a fool of yourself," said Durwood. "So many people are too neurotic. They're afraid to take risks. I had good people and educated friends come up and ask me with that haunting refrain: 'What if it fails?'

"And I would tell them if I don't try, it already has."

He embarked on his great Toe Floss adventure with a pioneer's spirit. He wasn't sure what was up ahead – a learning curve or dead man's curve.

Tommy stayed late at the office one night, writing and designing a brochure for Toe Floss.

"Everybody loved it, but it was verbose and over-written," Tommy said, laughing. "All the information could have easily been condensed to a single page."

Toe Floss made its stage debut at a trade show in July 1977 at the Atlanta Merchandise Mart. Durwood and Tommy rented a booth and loaded up their cars with Toe Floss.

Optimism was at an all-time high.

"What if we don't have enough pencils to take down all the orders?" Durwood asked his friend.

Said Tommy: "I hope that's a problem."

They had a chair shaped like a hand. A friend had also loaned them a large mechanical hand. They put a canister of Toe Floss in the hand and placed it on a revolving turntable.

It became the hand that would feed them. By the end of the trade show, they had sold 2,160 boxes of Toe Floss at $1 each.

Durwood hawked it like a traveling salesman. On Aug. 16, 1977, he went on WSB-TV to promote it. The television station had interviewed some contestants in the Miss Georgia pageant, which was a difficult act to follow. That was the least of his problems. The station had intended to introduce him as the "Toe Floss King." But that idea was quickly nixed.

Another King was dead. It was the day Elvis Presley died.

While he got an "A" for effort, he didn't get many points for etiquette when he showed up unannounced at the front offices of Rich's department store with a box of Toe Floss.

He didn't have an appointment. He was wearing sneakers and blue jeans. The odds were stacked against him getting past the first line of defense – the office secretary.

The manager of the "notions" department had his door open. He overheard Durwood's sales pitch, and his curiosity nudged him into the hallway.

"The way I went about it was categorically wrong," said Durwood. "But he was fascinated with it. He told me later he knew after two minutes I wasn't a con man. He said I was 'deliciously naïve.'

"Some people never proceed because they don't have any guarantees. But I think there's a lot to be said for blind faith. I didn't know anybody in the business. The idea of not knowing how to do it right certainly didn't keep me from trying."

Gene Mori was just as enthused with the novelty of Toe Floss.

He owned and operated Mori's Luggage & Gifts along with his wife, Betty, the sister of Georgia Senator Sam Nunn.

"He put out the edict that he wanted it next to all the cash registers at his stores," said Durwood. "It was the perfect impulse buy. Nobody was going to go into a store looking for Toe Floss. I sold them to him for 75 cents each, and he sold them for $1.50. It became my bread-and-butter account.

"I'll never forget the first invoice I sent. I faxed it to him, and he faxed me back a check. We did this a couple of times before I caught on. I called him up and said: 'You don't care for faxes, do you?' "

Toe Floss became his calling card. The front of the container read: "Furwood Dincher's Original Toe Floss for prompt, temporary relief of foot in mouth." The bottom of the label read: "approved by at least one podiatrist."

There was a certain amount of truth in advertising. Durwood had met a podiatrist named Mark Rappoport. The good-natured foot doctor had agreed to put his anonymous stamp of approval on the novelty product.

The back of each container hailed Toe Floss as the "ultimate bathroom buff" and espoused its benefits as the "world's only 'footifrice,' developed after years of intensive research. ... Studies show it to be an effective mildew and dry-rot preventative when used in a conscientiously applied program of daily foot hygiene."

Also included were these directions for use:

Standard Method: Having soaped and rinsed the feet thoroughly in warm water, cut a 6-inch length of Toe Floss and draw it lightly between the toes. Stubborn food particles, barnacles and rust spots may require extra attention.

Overnight Method: Tie a 4-inch length of the floss around each toe and leave on overnight to absorb the infectious material which naturally accumulates during sleep.

To Remove Foot from Mouth: Tie a 2-inch length of Toe Floss around the affected ankle and apply firm but steady traction. The foot will gradually slip out and should be flossed vigorously to prevent possible infection. Chronic foot-in-mouth may require the attention of a qualified podiatrist.

Durwood later wrote a check to Schiffman to repay his debt, but Schiffman tore up the check.

"Toe Floss wasn't an assurance of big-time money but it provided the next step," said Durwood. "It was the financial bridge that afforded me the opportunity to stop teaching because at least I had some kind of income. I really do believe it kept my mind from being cluttered by worrying about how I was going to pay the rent. It became part of who I was. I eventually worked it into my speaking routine, and I learned how to market it. Attitude is everything, just like the little train. I think I can. I think I can."

Soon, that foot in the mouth would help him get his foot in the door.

Ella Mae at Christmas, wearing one of her favorite dresses.
(Photo courtesy of Durwood Fincher.)

Stairway to heaven

Ella Mae Fincher was a strong woman. She could stand her ground. There wasn't much she couldn't handle.

She was fearless.

But she did have her fears.

Among the things that terrified her were escalators. She suffered from "escalaphobia" and there wasn't anything in Dr. Meriwether's medicine bag that could cure it.

"She didn't like moving objects," said Durwood. "I tried to tell her she didn't have to jump on them, just step. But she couldn't grasp that concept. She just knew it was moving, and she wasn't buckled in. She would get nervous and take the elevator."

She would break into a cold sweat at the sight – or even the very thought – of merging onto those grooved steps. In her nightmares she would be confronted with sharp, metal teeth that would appear and disappear, with the sliding handrails.

Durwood did everything he could to calm her fear. He would take her downtown to Newberry's department store to "practice" riding the escalators.

It was a classic case of role reversal. It was like a child teaching his parent how to ride a bicycle.

It did not work. It was frustrating.

"I love you, Mama," Durwood told her. "But this does not make me proud."

Ella Mae rarely confronted the other flights of fright scattered through her life. Among them was the fear of being swallowed by the big city. She was not fond of Atlanta. It was like a thousand moving escalators. She merely tolerated it because Durwood lived there.

After all, she had spent most of her life in the village, where the streets were narrow and the tallest buildings rarely rose above attic level. Just driving herself from Macon to Statesboro had been a major ordeal. She was not fond of it, and it became a fear that had to be conquered.

She had her own peculiar way of dealing with her "Atlantaphobia." Whether she drove herself there or had Roy take her, she would never wade too deep. They would find a parking lot on the outskirts of the city and wait for Durwood to pick them up and carry them into the concrete jungle.

One of the few exceptions was when they would travel to an Atlanta Braves game. Ella Mae was a huge fan of the perennial cellar-dwellers. She was deeply devoted to her boys of summer. She followed them religiously on her transistor radio, listening to the familiar broadcasting team of Milo Hamilton, Ernie Johnson and, later, Skip Caray.

The Braves usually were buried in or near last place by the time the final Georgia peach had been plucked from the orchards in early August. By then, as Caray used to say, thousands of fans would show up "disguised as empty seats." By Labor Day, most Atlantans had turned their thoughts from cowhide to pigskin. Baseball moved over, and King Football took center stage.

Ella Mae's aversion to driving into Atlanta was met with an asterisk. She felt safe pulling into the shadows of Atlanta-Fulton County Stadium, not far from the gold dome of the state capitol. Although the stadium was surrounded by some of south Atlanta's least-desirable neighborhoods, she usually could find a good parking spot, especially late in the season.

So, on Saturday night, Sept. 9, 1978, Roy and Katherine accompanied her to Atlanta to watch the Braves play Los Angeles. They met Durwood at the stadium. The Braves won 7-4, behind the pitching of Phil Niekro, one of Ella Mae's favorite players.

So Ella Mae was happy. Roy was happy. Katherine was happy. And Durwood was happy. He walked them to their car in the parking lot. It was Ella Mae's new Dodge, the first new car she had ever owned. The car cost more than her house in the village.

Roy took the keys and got ready to take her on the 80-mile trip back to Macon. Ella Mae would return to Statesboro the next day to prepare for the start of fall classes at Georgia Southern.

Ella Mae wasn't much on farewells. She would wrap her arms around you and smother you with kisses, but the word "good-bye" rarely crossed her lips.

So there was no benediction as the stars lifted their chins above the Atlanta skyline.

"I love you, Mama," Durwood said to the most important person in his life.

Of course, he had no way of knowing it would be the last time he would ever see her. It would be the last time his ears would hear her voice, dripping with the sweetness of honeysuckle.

Duh-wood.

On Monday morning, he was in his classroom at Westminster. The call came to the front office. A student monitor was sent to watch Durwood's classroom, which was located near the auditorium.

"Walking up there, I knew something had to be wrong," said Durwood.

The headmaster closed the door. There was a tremor in his voice.

"You need to call your brother," he told Durwood.

Durwood dialed the number: 912-745-9826.

Katherine answered.

"Roy and I think you should come home," she said. "Could you do that?"

It was an Indian Summer day. September had arrived, but summer had lingered. The temperature had climbed into the 90s in Statesboro.

Although it was cooler inside the air-conditioned dormitories at Georgia Southern, Ella Mae couldn't shoo the heat away from her body. She was perspiring as she walked into a meeting for the house directors.

"Isn't it hot?" she announced.

Then she put her head on the table and took her final breath of Georgia air.

She was only 58 years old.

Durwood rode to Statesboro with Roy and Katherine to gather Ella Mae's belongings.

Louise Screws, director of housing at Georgia Southern, comforted Durwood by telling him his mother had died with a smile on her face.

"If you could ever choose the way you wanted to leave this earthly place that would be it. It was all so gentle," Louise said.

They turned the key to the lock on her door and went in her room. Everything was just the way she had left it that morning, as if it were waiting for her to come back. There was half a glass of orange juice in the refrigerator.

Although it was painful for Durwood, he took comfort in knowing those nine years in Statesboro had been some of the most memorable times of her life. She had lived in beautiful, stately buildings. She had been close to the library, and she went there every day.

She adored the students, faculty and community. The feeling was mutual.

Her death was newsworthy enough to merit a 164-word article on the front page of the Statesboro Herald. The story referred to her as a "house mom" to some 2,000 students at the college.

Her Dodge still had the new-car smell. Durwood drove it back to Macon, pausing in almost every little town along the way to wipe his tears.

She had left strict instructions to Roy and Durwood about her funeral. Under no circumstances was there to be an open casket. She wanted a graveside service. She asked them to keep it simple. Her favorite scripture, Romans 8:28, was to be read.

They followed the black hearse as it left Hart's Mortuary in downtown Macon. On those same streets where she had built her life and raised her family, people stopped to pay their respects.

"That touched me," said Durwood. "They didn't even know her, and they pulled their cars over to the side of the road. She deserved that much."

Ella Mae was laid to rest at Macon Memorial Park. There were mourners from Bellevue Baptist, the church she had joined when she was 14 years old. They came from the village, too. Neighbors who shared their front porches and toiled elbow to elbow in the cotton mill, showed up to pay their respects. There was also a contingent from Georgia Southern.

Durwood appreciated the comforting words and condolences. But the sound of the pine trees swaying in the wind reminded him of the time his mother had told him about her own mother and father's funerals.

She had talked about the empty sound of the wind as it brushed against the pine trees. It was the saddest sound she had ever heard, and she carried it with her.

Durwood would carry it with him, too.

He missed his mama.

If there was an "up" escalator to heaven, no doubt Ella Mae was on it.

Roses on Ella Mae's headstone at Macon Memorial Park on the 30th anniversary of her death in 2008. (Photo by Ed Grisamore.)

"I've got to find an audience. And I've got to get an audience to find me."
(Illustration courtesy of Durwood Fincher.)

Good thing he believed in free speech

To his friends in the village, he was always at the front of the line for casting. He had all the words memorized. He was the guy who came back for curtain calls.

To his classmates at Georgia Southern, he was an emcee on the stage of life. They figured he would go on to become the next Red Skelton. Give that man a microphone. Put a star on his dressing room door.

To the students he taught at Hardaway and Westminster, he could take the ordinary and make it extraordinary. There was magic in his method.

The big top? All he needed was a break.

Durwood had a college degree to hang on his wall and lots of friends to sit on his furniture. The nominal success of Toe Floss had ensured, at least for the time being, there wouldn't be too much month at the end of the money. He had taken the $16,000 he inherited from Ella Mae's life insurance policy, bought some stock in AT&T and built a tiny nest egg. He never went for the fast cars and wild women, so it was enough to sustain him.

He didn't have it all, nor did he want it all.

But he wanted more.

"I've got to find an audience," he told himself. "And I've got to get an audience to find me."

He was still honing his doubletalking skills on parking attendants, grocery store clerks and dinner party guests. But he longed to get in front of a wider audience.

So he began to market himself. Shameless self-promotion. He

wrote letters on a small Royal typewriter. He addressed them to program chairmen for civic clubs and ladies in charge of their church senior groups.

He begged. He pleaded. *Look at me!*

"It was like fishing," he said. "You get one bite every 10 times you put your line in the water. I would tell them I had developed a routine. My sales pitch was everybody loves a surprise. I didn't use the word 'imposter.' But I fell in love with the idea of fooling people in a good way."

He began to make his rounds on the fried chicken circuit, choking down cold dinner rolls in banquet rooms at the Holiday Inn and nibbling on every casserole prepared by the ladies auxiliary at the Methodist church.

He knew these groups didn't pay. They would shake his hand afterward and tell him they hoped he had enjoyed his lunch. Every now and then, they might slip him a small honorarium or love offering to help put some unleaded in the Corolla.

It's a good thing he believed in free speech. He sure gave enough of them.

Years later he would meet author Herb Cohen, who gave him a great line about honorariums.

"More honor," laughed Herb, "than rarium."

He kept telling himself patience is a virtue.

"It was like developing a photograph," said Durwood. "It takes time before it becomes a picture. Those were lean years, the salad days. Someone would call every couple of months and ask me to speak, so I was only doing about six or nine speeches a year. I began to realize that, even if I had gotten $10,000 for every speech I made, it wasn't going to work unless I started getting some volume."

One day – he can't remember if it was the Kiwanis club or the Rotary – he let loose his doubletalk and looked out into a sea of whiplashed faces, not realizing his first meal ticket was seated at one of the tables.

Margaret and Dupree Jordan were in the audience. They would become pilgrims on his journey.

The husband-and-wife team ran Jordan Enterprises, a small marketing, public relations and speakers bureau from a cramped office on Maple Drive in Buckhead.

"It was just a little mom-and-pop shop, like an upholstery place," said Durwood.

When the Jordans heard him speak that day, they got his name and number from one of the officers with the civic club and called him.

Dupree had once been a speaker himself. And a preacher.

He had been around long enough to tell a contender from a pretender, even if it was on a much smaller scale.

"He could see I was just starting out, but I had a routine that was different, and I think that's what got him," said Durwood. "It wasn't the same old thing. They had booked enough salesmen and wannabe comedians who sold insurance and real estate. I was young. I had taught school. And Dupree liked me."

Margaret Jordan also was fond of Durwood. If they were going to take a chance on him, she had one stipulation.

"She wanted to make sure my act was clean," said Durwood. "I wasn't offended when she told me that, but it was almost like my aunt talking to me. I understood her concern. Their name and reputation were on the line."

They booked him for what they called their "annual showcase." It was pretty much an amateur hour. Different groups could attend the luncheon and get a sampling of speakers auditioning for keynote addresses and corporate dinners.

The showcase began to open a few more doors. There was no windfall, but the phone began to ring a little more frequently.

One day, it was Jordan. It was the summer of 1981.

"We've got you a show in Cincinnati," he said. "It pays $275."

Durwood could hardly contain his excitement.

"I'll be on the next plane," he said.

The group was executives from Texaco Oil who had gathered at the Salt Fork State Lodge, northeast of Cincinnati.

Durwood promised Dupree he would make them laugh. He would have them falling out of their chairs and screaming for more.

Behind the scenes, though, it would be a comedy of errors.

The man who would later become one of the most experienced travelers of his generation – with almost six million sky miles on Delta – was quite the accidental tourist.

He piled his clothes into a suitcase, rushed to the airport, squeezed into a seat in "coach" and buckled up for the 80-minute flight.

His heart raced through the clouds with him. The turbulence started when he landed.

Durwood went to the Hertz counter to rent a car for the drive to Salt Fork.

He had money. He had brought his checkbook.

But he had forgotten his driver's license.

"I can't rent you a car without your license," said the young woman behind the counter. "It is the state law."

He had never felt so dumb in his life. He asked her to trust him. Didn't he have an honest face? When he got back, he would send her a nice tip.

"No," she said. "I'm very sorry."

He took a cab. He sat in the back seat.

"The whole way I kept telling myself I probably needed to go back to teaching," he said.

He remains forever grateful to the taxi driver who accepted his personal check without any proof of identification.

"The first big gig of my career was saved by a nameless cab driver," he said.

But his performance was a smash success. He looks back now and realizes how primitive his speech must have been. He had no track record. His past was thin. He had no video to show them.

He did have a slight problem at the end of the night, though. He needed to get back to the airport.

As luck would have it, and he sure needed some, one of the band members hired for the event was driving back to Cincinnati in the morning.

Durwood never forgot his license again.

Live and learn, he told himself. Live and learn.

Sometimes you wonder if the speaker you hire is going to make any sense. Not with DURWOOD FINCHER — He never makes sense.

He's been called "Mr. Doubletalk" by *Candid Camera's* Allen Funt. Corporate executives have called him "the great imposter" and "the perfect icebreaker." Who knows what you'll call him, but you'll agree that Durwood Fincher is like no other speaker in America today.

He's usually introduced as Dr. Rayford S. Bundy, a highly-touted government "expert" straight from Washington. His speech, custom-tailored to your theme or requirements, is a delicious diatribe filled with bureaucratic rhetoric and platitudes and delivered with that all-too-familiar boring speaker's monotone.

"Oh, no!" the audience thinks to itself as the sentences grow longer and the words become more obscure. Soon everyone is squirming and frowning as "words" begin to appear that really aren't words at all.

Suddenly, someone realizes what's happening and snickers. Then two or three others catch on and begin to chuckle. Finally, a wave of realization passes over the audience, and frowns turn into laughter as everyone becomes aware that he or she has been "had."

Recognizing that he has been "discovered," Durwood concludes on a positive note that leaves your people relieved, relaxed, and ready to get the most out of the remainder of your meeting.

Confused? No need to be. We have ½" VHS and ¾" video cassettes available so you can see and hear for yourself why Durwood Fincher is called upon again and again to start major corporate meetings off on the right foot. No matter what the purpose or topic of your meeting, Durwood can prime your audience to a high level of receptiveness so they can benefit most from your presentation.

Call or write today for more information on America's most unique speaker — Durwood Fincher.

DURWOOD FINCHER
Suite 200, 1605 Chantilly Drive, N.E., Atlanta, Georgia 30324
Phone (404) 329-0620

One of vintage Mr. Doubletalk's promotional brochures.
(Photo courtesy of Durwood Fincher.)

Whatever it was, he wanted to be ready for it. (Illustration by Bryan Hendrix.)

Come on, something!

There always would be a "Tom" in his life. Maybe it was because "Tom" was part of his middle name. Durwood Tomlinson Fincher.

At Hardaway he was Tom Cohen's STAR teacher. Cohen has remained his close friend, his lawyer and business manager.

In his early days in Atlanta, Durwood met Tommy Teaver, a gifted musician and half of the brains behind Toe Floss.

There was Tom Kearns, too. They met when Kearns was running for the board of directors of the condominium association where Durwood lives. Kearns later helped develop Durwood's website and managed his schedule.

But perhaps the king of the Tom Boys was Tom Little.

There was nothing little about him. He was a giant.

Durwood dreamed of breaking into the advertising field, and Little was a partner in McDonald & Little, one of the major advertising firms in the South.

Mike McDonald was a Harvard grad, and Tom Little was a barbecue man from Birmingham. It turned out to be a perfect combination. McDonald had the business brains. Little had the personality.

"He's the most creative person I've ever known," Durwood said. "He was a genius, the kind of guy I wanted to hang around."

Little once won a Clio Award – the advertising world's equivalent of an Oscar or Grammy – for a famous commercial he created for Piedmont Airlines.

In the commercial, a traveler makes his way through first class on an airplane, where the passengers – beautiful people dressed in white – are being wined and dined. When the curtain is pulled to the "coach" section, he is shown to his seat with the immigrants, goats and pigs. A dirge is being played on a hand-cranked phonograph.

The commercial made its point. There was no distinction between "first class" and "coach" at the airline. All passengers were treated equally.

Little also was the brains behind the name of a new citrus-flavored, caffeine soft drink. It was developed by Atlanta-based Coca-Cola in 1979 to compete with Pepsi's popular Mountain Dew.

Little proposed the name "Mello Yello" to company executives. He later would describe that meeting as talking to a "table of suits." Most of them loved it. One man, however, was concerned Mello Yello sounded too much like a psychedelic drug.

"Is that so?" said Little, tugging on his cigarette. "Ever heard of Coke?"

Durwood met Little through Rebecca Johnson, who had taken over her father's publishing company, which produced Pecan South magazine. She let Durwood have some office space for his Toe Floss operation.

Her husband, Mark, was a partner in an advertising company. Mark had gotten Durwood to speak to a Federal Express group in Memphis early in his speaking career. He and Rebecca invited Durwood to a party at their house.

It was a chance to network. At the party, Durwood was introduced to Sue Deer, who worked as a publicist for the High Museum of Art. Durwood also got to meet Tom Little and his wife, Sandy.

"Tom took a liking to me," Durwood said. "I wasn't looking for a job. He just liked me. At that point, I was unemployed. I was living off my inheritance from my mother and whatever I could make on the Toe Floss."

Little eventually moved to New York to try to secure a stronghold in advertising there, but it didn't work out. He stayed close to Durwood, and asked him to go with him and Sandy to Baltimore to work for an ad agency there. After a month, that didn't work out either. So they returned to Atlanta, where he opened the Thomas Stinson Little agency at Piedmont Crossing.

"He told me he wanted me to work for him, and I asked him what I would do," said Durwood. "He said we would figure it out as we went along."

Durwood answered the phone and was the office gopher. (He would "go-fer" this and "go-fer" that.) Little had a business card that identified him as "President of TSL." Durwood created his own business card. His title was "Friend of the President."

Like Durwood, Ken Crooms had grown up in Macon. Age and geography had kept their paths from crossing, but their universes came together at Little's office.

Ken worked for Lanier Business Products and had sold a copier to Little. His territory ranged from Buckhead to Spaghetti Junction.

"I would stop by their office on my lunch break," Ken said. "Durwood was like a receptionist. He would answer the phone. It was always so much fun to watch him if a telemarketer called. He would put them on hold and hit the speakerphone for the entire office. He would announce to everybody he had a telemarketer on Line 2. If they wanted to listen, come on up to the front."

Then he would pull the trigger on his doubletalk.

"One time a lady called selling magazine subscriptions," said Ken. "He started doubletalking her and told her he had just inherited several million dollars from his aunt. He was interested in investing in the magazine company. When she said she would go get her manager, he would start doubletalking again. We would be in the background trying to hold back the laughter."

Sometimes, Ken would help him wrap Toe Floss in the conference room during his lunch break.

Durwood always seemed to have plenty of it. In fact, he had so much at his house, he decided to put it to good use one Halloween.

There was a costume party at the Fox Theatre. Durwood had an idea.

"I didn't have a costume, but I had all this Toe Floss," he said. "I took a cornucopia and tied it onto my face with all the rope to make a beak. I put on a wig and a jacket with a scarf and big gloves. I was so covered you couldn't even tell I was white.

"When we got to the Fox, there were people parading around in $500 costumes, things you see at Mardi Gras.''

As soon as the judging began, Durwood found himself among the 10 finalists. After another round of voting, he made the cut to the top five.

Bob Van Camp, who played the famous "Mighty Mo" organ at the Fox, was serving as the emcee. He went up to each of the finalists on stage and asked about their costume.

"I was just lowballing it with that outfit,'' said Durwood. "But when he got to me, I leaned toward him and said: 'Hey, man, I'm just a bird, and I'm glad to be here.'''

The applause was deafening. Durwood won first prize.

"The check was for $30 and the sponsor was from Macon,'' he said. "I don't remember his name, but I do remember the check bounced. I hated that because I really needed the money.''

There were some things about Tom Little that Durwood had to overlook. He was a chain smoker. He was married five times. He gave up so many houses and so much furniture he would tell people, "If I knew then what I know now, I would have rented shoes.''

But his advice was sage. Most of it still echoes in Durwood's ears.

"He used to say to never let 'em see your warts,'' said Durwood. "Come in, trick 'em, make 'em laugh and get out of there.''

He had cancer. On his deathbed, he called Durwood to his side.

"I liked you because you never wanted anything,'' he told Durwood. "You were always just glad to be there. So I want to leave you with a line I've never used. It's three of the simplest words ever bumped together.

"COME ON, SOMETHING!!!''

Durwood thought about it. He would be thinking about it for the rest of his life.

Come on, something!!! It didn't really matter what "something'' was, just that it came.

"Come on, something!!!'' Little said. "You can have it. It belongs to you.''

A month later, he died.

"I believe, with all my heart, my mother always had known 'something' was coming for me," Durwood said. "She knew something grand was brewing that was bigger than both of us. And she wanted to make sure I was ready for whatever it was."

Advertising guru Tom Little was a huge creative influence on Durwood. (Photo courtesy of Mark and Rebecca Johnson.)

The late Allen Funt, creator and host of "Candid Camera," is credited with giving Durwood his name, "Mr. Doubletalk." (Photo courtesy of Allen Funt Productions.)

The snort heard round the room

He built his career on nebulous nonsense, jittery jabberwocky and frenetic phonetics.

But one sound rose above the others.

It was the sound a secretary made on a spring afternoon in 1981.

Time has erased her name and her face, but nothing will erase the sound that rose from her throat one day at the Wyndham Hotel in Vinings, north of Atlanta.

It wasn't a word. It was a reaction, a response.

Phhhhlllllluuuungggggfffff.

He made her laugh. The man she worked for, Allen Funt, had grown weary of the stream of aspiring comedians who had paraded past his table.

Durwood was one of hundreds of people to audition for the legendary creator and host of the Candid Camera television show. Funt had been hired by IBM to cast about 30 people for company videos. The search was on to find a comic personality to do candid interviews with IBM employees and add some humor to corporate meetings at Big Blue.

By the time Funt got to Durwood, though, he had been pistol-whipped. So he never even realized it when Durwood pulled the pin on his devious doubletalk and launched it like a live grenade into his lap.

"Sure," Funt responded, his glasses low on the bridge of his nose. "OK. All right. Nice to ... er, meet you."

Then the secretary giggled. Actually, it was a snort.

Phhhhlllllluuuungggggfffff.

In many ways it all went back to Dupree and Margaret Jordan.

They had opened a door that led to other doors, and Durwood kept reaching for those doorknobs. One of them came when the Jordans introduced him to an Atlanta talent agent.

She landed him a part in a commercial for Crystal lemonade. She also encouraged him to throw his hat in the ring for the IBM gig. Of course, it could be like standing in a long line to ride the Scream Machine at Six Flags, but it might parlay into something.

"I don't know exactly what they're looking for," she told him. "But it's some kind of routine where the person can do some gibberish. Do you feel confident enough to try it?"

"If nothing else, I would love to go just to meet Allen Funt," said Durwood.

Had the order of auditions been alphabetical, Durwood might have had the benefit of a semi-fresh Funt. But the line was moving randomly, the numbers jumbled. By the time Durwood's name was called, Funt was clamoring for the exits.

"It was early American Idol – without the singing," said Durwood. "I was either going to get the part or get thrown out of there."

He knew he had to have a hook, a gimmick to separate him from the rest of the pack of no-hit wonders.

"Mr. Funt," he said, introducing himself, "before we get started, do you think it's possible if we *iree-stineck-adorevesen* and add that to the notion of *marrol-keenoo-kono-sofoh?*"

"Why, yes, of course," said Funt. His hands were sorting through a stack of folders, but his mind was obviously elsewhere.

Then came the snort heard round the room.

The secretary giggled.

Phhhhhlllllluuuuunggggffffff.

It registered about a 7.4 on the snicker scale.

If only Durwood remembered her name, knew where she lived and had kept up with her all these years, he could thank her. He could send her roses and boxes of chocolate. He could smother her cheek with kisses of gratitude. He could give her a big bonus at Christmas.

"Her reaction is what did it," Durwood said. "Mr. Funt realized I had done something to make her laugh. It was like she was telling him: 'Oh, he got you good, Allen.' For me, that moment will always be frozen in time. I was standing there. My knees were knocking. A look came over his face. 'I'm Allen Funt, and he got me!' "

Funt had made a living out of catching unsuspecting people "in the act of being themselves." He prided himself more in being an astute observer of human nature than a practical joker.

The tables had been turned.

"I think we've found our man," he told his assistant.

The name at the top of the form said "Durwood Fincher" but Funt largely ignored it.

"Mr. Doubletalk," he said. "We'll call him Mr. Doubletalk."

From "IBMSpeak" to "Doubletalk," Durwood had a good ride with Big Blue.
(Photo courtesy of Durwood Fincher.)

Big Blue

In the business world, IBM meant International Business Machines.

But, inside one of the country's largest companies, it meant "I've Been Moved." There was lots of movement up and down the corporate ladders at Big Blue.

In 1981, IBM added two more letters to the American landscape. It introduced what was called the "PC," for Personal Computer. The PC became the standard of the industry and started a technology revolution of "IBM-compatible" computers and software.

By the following year, "Time" magazine had chosen the "Personal Computer" as its "Man of the Year."

IBM had lots of money and lots of people.

But, Durwood could sense, not enough fun.

"They loved me because of the doubletalk," he said. "IBM was notorious for what was known as IBMSpeak. Back then, IBM was so large it wasn't a company. It was a nation."

The corporation also was going through some difficult changes. Many of the company's almost 365,000 employees were uptight about their job security.

"The complexion was changing because we were going through some of our first layoffs at that time," said Bob Colby, an executive producer for IBM's "recognition" events. "All of a sudden, it wasn't the womb-to-tomb job it had been in the past."

Durwood was brought in as a corporate comedian to lighten things up. But, when Funt delivered Durwood to IBM, Bob wasn't sure what to think.

"He said, 'We've got Mr. Doubletalk here,' and nobody was quite sure what that meant," Bob said. "At first I thought Durwood might just be a one horse-and-pony thing. Once people have seen the gig, you can't really do it again. But we were charged with the idea to see if we could find other places to fit in Durwood."

In the stiff-collared corporate world, the company's thousands of employees got to see Durwood in his tenderfoot days. And they appreciated the frivolity of his video interviews.

Here was this tower of babble, with muttonchops running down his cheeks, making no sense as he rambled and hurled a string of frazzled consonants and vowels at puzzled employees.

The earliest interviews borrowed a page right out of "Candid Camera." Shots were done with a hidden camera while Durwood was equipped with a hidden microphone.

"We didn't want people to know they were being taped so they wouldn't immediately know he was putting them on," Bob said. "He would grab people at these 'recognition' meetings and start asking nonsensical questions. He would tell them he was doing a survey. At one point, we either brought out the camera or somebody saw it and asked if we were taping. We found that when people knew they were on camera they tried even harder to understand what he was talking about. That worked to our advantage because people didn't want to look like idiots on tape."

The IBM brass loved Durwood's routines and challenged Bob and his staff to come up with even more creative ways to get him on the programs. He would shuttle back and forth between the Fountainbleau Hotel in Miami and Mark Hopkins Hotel in San Francisco.

He would be introduced as the company's new marketing guru. Or he might pose as a sports director for a TV station. Or a chef back in the kitchen. Or the pilot who was scheduled to fly them home.

"Durwood was a genuinely funny man," Bob said. "Even without the doubletalk, he was hilarious. We started to push the envelope with him, and he pushed it with us. We would say: 'Let's try this' and he would say: 'Let's try that' and it really developed.

"Everybody was so used to a motivational speaker or a business speaker or an accountant. Durwood gave them permission to laugh at themselves.''

They would nod and giggle. *Yep, sounds just like IBMSpeak. This guy might not be playing our song, but he is speaking our language.* Durwood also would have fun with his version of "sniglets," a poplar expression at the time for words that should appear in the dictionary, but don't.

At Colby's suggestion, he began expanding his "candid camera" roles to include infiltrating company events.

It was a challenge, but at least Durwood had plenty of experience. The Great Imposter had been "crashing" parties for years.

"I would go to these social functions, and they would have these beautiful spreads of food," he said. "Everybody would be dressed up, and I would come in wearing a sports coat with a pair of shorts. I looked like I had just wandered in off the beach.

"I would load up a big plate of food, and everybody would watch me. I wasn't gross or a slob. I would just go around telling people how nice it was that IBM had all this food for everybody. Then someone would come up and say: 'Well, it's not for everybody! This is not for the public.' I would offer to pay, but they would tell me no. We got it all on camera.''

Wherever IBM went, Mr. Doubletalk followed. To hotels. To convention centers. To casinos.

"At one point they booked me for three months and were paying me $750 a day," he said. "That first check I got from IBM was for $28,000. I could not imagine making that kind of money. My first year teaching at Hardaway, I made $4800. There was indeed a Santa Claus.

"Do you remember years ago Xerox had the commercials where the priest was their miracle?" Durwood said. "Well, IBM was *my* miracle. They saturated me. I was doing 30-40 shows a year. I was making good money. I also looked at it as the best investment I ever made.''

The "investment" began to pay even bigger dividends. He had become well known within the company. But an even bigger break came when he was allowed inside the "main tent." He was hired to do an IBM dealers' meeting at the Marriott Hotel in San Diego. There were 1,800 people there, representing fledgling companies like Microsoft that had their own meetings and conventions. These were companies that were looking for entertainers and speakers.

The circle was beginning to grow.

Back in the village, the speed limit was still 15 m.p.h. on the street where he grew up.

But that was long ago and far away. Durwood had found the fast lane.

It was way too fast.

Durwood being interviewed on the set by Bill Tush of WTBS in Atlanta.
(Photo courtesy of WTBS.)

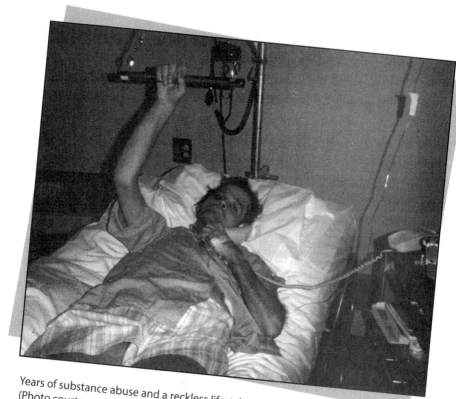

Years of substance abuse and a reckless lifestyle nearly cost Durwood his life. (Photo courtesy of Betty Cabaniss.)

Dark side of the moon

He never drank or smoked cigarettes. In high school and college, he couldn't afford it. When his buddies would light Marlboros, then pass around mugs of Budweiser and shots of Jim Beam, he would allow himself an occasional sip or swallow.

But he never acquired a taste for Schlitz, and he never ran with Jack Daniels.

After college, he began smoking marijuana. He felt the burn of the rolling paper as it pressed against his lips. It didn't take long for the "high" to sweep over him. It was fun to ruffle life's edges, if only with a temporary pass.

Then Ella Mae died and turned his world upside down.

He started making a lot of money and traveling for the first time in his career. He began to hang around big wigs and jet setters at lavish parties, where temptation was passed around like finger food.

Cocaine called his name. Nose candy. He watched as others snorted it up their nostrils and rubbed the fine white powder against their gums.

He got caught up in it, too. He played with that fire.

It almost killed him.

"There were two forces in my life," he said. "I had come from nothing. But I had started to do well enough with my routine, and I had this newness of wealth.

"I also had lost my mama, and I was going into the depths of depression. That combination triggered it. I fell for cocaine."

Betty Cabaniss could see the tell-tale signs. She was the mother of Danny Cabaniss, his former student at Hardaway. She had moved back to Atlanta after her divorce.

"I wanted to help Durwood because we had been so close in Columbus," she said. "But I would go over to his house, and he would lock me out. He wouldn't talk on the telephone. He was so confused. He was shutting everybody out, even those who cared about him."

"I was out of control and didn't care," he said. "Later, I would have all the guilt in the world over what I had done to myself. I remember thinking: 'Oh, Mama, I'm so glad you didn't have to see this.'"

In February 1983, a former student from Westminster dropped by Durwood's house on West Wieuca. He found Durwood in the bed. Durwood had used cocaine earlier in the day. His whole body hurt. He thought he had the flu and said he needed to go to the hospital. When he was admitted, he was told he had "everything except the flu."

He was suffering from pneumonia and bacterial endocarditis, an inflammation of the heart's inner lining. There was a massive staph infection from drug use that had spread systematically across his body and was primarily in his lungs.

It was life-threatening. The doctor listed Durwood's odds of survival at about 14 percent then lowered it to 8 percent.

Roy and Katherine were contacted at their home in Macon. They were told Durwood had been admitted at Piedmont Hospital.

He was in intensive care.

He was not expected to live.

"When we saw him, his eyes were big, and he wasn't breathing on his own," said Katherine. "He looked like he was scared to death. He was lying there dying. Roy and I asked him if he had any life insurance. We needed to know if there was anything we should do. He was in so deep, nobody was expecting him to get out."

There are only pockets of memory of that winter and early spring. The room stayed dark. Nurses moved in and out. Doctors shook their heads in silence as they viewed his charts.

He could hear the monitors beeping above his head. He was aware of the rise and fall of his chest beneath the ventilator. There was the steady drip of the IV machine.

No one was allowed to visit him in his room without wearing

a mask.

One night he ended up code blue. He was hooked up to the ventilator. It was doing the breathing for him. He dreamed the tubes coming out of his mouth were snakes, and he reached up to rip them out of his mouth.

"I think every alarm in ICU went off," he said. "I looked up and there must have been 18 people in that room. They thought something catastrophic had happened."

Betty went to see him every day. She was a psychiatric nurse who worked at another hospital.

"I really thought he was going to die. I never prayed so hard in my life," she said. "I cried when I went to see him in ICU. The doctor came out and asked if I was family. I told him I was as close as he had right now. He said he thought I should know this man had about an 8 percent chance of surviving.

"And I said, 'Well, he can't die. We can't let him die. He is important to so many people.' I told the doctor Durwood didn't have much insurance, but I would sell my house to save him. The doctor told me it wasn't a matter of money. He was just that sick.

"When his brother had asked if he had any life insurance, he meant to say health insurance. But, when you only have an 8 percent chance of living, life insurance is what you probably should be talking about. Who's gonna buy the casket?"

It would be a long time before Betty saw any signs of encouragement. The jolly man the doctors had called "Buddha" was down to 156 pounds.

"He looked like a skeleton," Betty said. "I was working the night shift, so I would stay with him for a couple of hours. I would go to work with tears in my eyes. I could not imagine life without Durwood."

Her ex-husband, Dan, was a prominent doctor in Columbus. He flew to Colorado, where Danny was living, and tried to prepare him for a funeral.

Danny's father was a cardiologist, so he was well aware of the seriousness of Durwood's condition.

"He gave me the statistics," Danny said. "He flew all the way out there because he knew how close I was to Durwood. And he told me he was there to tell me my friend was going to die.''

Durwood realized the error of his ways.

"Everything I had done was self-induced," he said. "Nobody had twisted my arm. Nobody had pulled out in front of me and caused me to have a wreck. I was there because of the choices I had made. Bad choices.

"Lying on the gurney that first night, I prayed like I had never prayed before," Durwood said. "I was down. I was dying. I prayed to the God I believe in. Openly, and without hesitation, I talked to Jesus. I made a commitment to God that if he allowed me to live through this situation I had brought upon myself, I would never touch cocaine again. It would never be a part of my life under any circumstances.''

His friends and family would come to visit. Sometimes he saw hope in their eyes. Sometimes he saw disappointment.

Slowly, Durwood began to turn one corner and then another. At first, food tasted metallic to him, but he finally began regaining his taste buds. Betty fed him ice cream and baked potatoes. She nursed him back to health on Tommy Teaver's tuna salad. When he started craving Chinese food, she drove across town to place an order.

There were setbacks, both mental and physical. At one point when he was getting better, he received some devastating news.

Jeff Singer and Susan Caulk had been two of his students at Westminster. Jeff had been Durwood's "one paid employee" at the Toe Floss factory on West Wieuca.

Jeff and Susan had gotten married about a year earlier. They had regularly come to visit Durwood in the hospital.

Durwood noticed they hadn't been by in several days, so he asked about them.

He was told they had been killed in a wreck near Helen. The car had gone over a cliff on a mountain road.

He spent three months in the hospital. His bill was in excess of $400,000.

"When he finally got out, he represented a victory for that hospital," said Betty. "Nobody thought he would live. The nurse who gave him rehab had told me she didn't know if she was ever going to get him to walk again. He was so resistant."

After his mother had died, Durwood had grown distant from his family in Macon. They had tried repeatedly to reconcile with him, but he shut them out. After he had shunned them, staying with Betty was his only option. So she took him home with her to nurse him back to health.

"All my friends thought I was nuts, and my mother was upset when I told her," Betty said. "Here I was taking in this strange, sorry guy who had nearly died from drugs."

She went to Druid Hills High School and put his name on the list for substitute teaching.

"There were times when I didn't think I was ever going to get him out of the house," she said. "One day he told me he hated me and threw a laundry basket at me. I told him I didn't care if he hated me. He had to do what I said and that was to get up off his butt and get a job."

Said Durwood: "That was the lowest low. I didn't have a house. I didn't have a car. I didn't have a job."

Years later he was at a private party. It was a beautiful home with two swimming pools. Durwood met a delightful couple. They remembered he was "Mr. Doubletalk." They had seen him on television. They knew nothing about his past.

The conversation was lively and fun. He made them laugh.

"I have some cocaine. Do you want to go up to the den and do a couple of lines?" the man asked Durwood.

Durwood told him no.

"You don't know what you're missing," the man said.

"Oh, I have a very vivid imagination," said Durwood. "Listen, I don't want to get into this with you. It's not the right place. But, for your own information, in the early 1980s I nearly died from a cocaine overdose. I was at a very bad place in my life. So, when I tell you I'm not going to do it tonight, I'm telling you I will never do it again. I was dying, and I made a vow before God."

The couple apologized and walked away. Two years later, Durwood ran into the woman at another party.

"I want you to know how much I appreciate your honesty that night," she told him. "Your story and your commitment made me think about it. I was never into anything like that, except socially. But I quit because I heard how you had started a little at a time and where it led."

He can now look back and reflect on his second chance.

Everybody deserves a second chance, but not everybody gets one. He knows that.

A friend asked him to speak at a drug rehabilitation center on the south side of Atlanta. The room was filled with men from all walks of life.

Durwood studied their sunken faces, the sharp lines in their skin. They were trying to come back, too.

He did his doubletalk routine. He made them laugh. He got them in a good mood.

And then he told them his story.

You could have heard a nod, a blink and a gulp. You could have heard the rustle of a toe against an insole.

"I know I am talking to a room full of recovering addicts, but I know where you are coming from," he said. "I was there. I have walked in your moccasins. And I'm living proof that you can change. It's never too late to get back on the path."

He remembered what his Grandma Tomlinson used to say.

If you don't stand for something, you'll fall for anything.

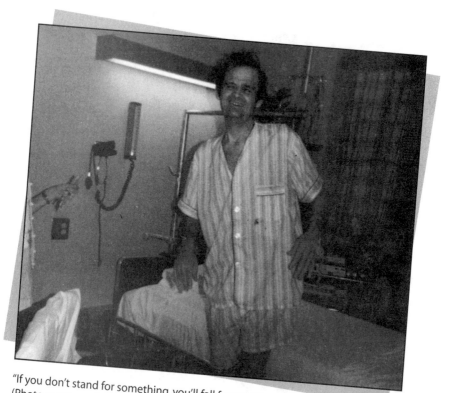

"If you don't stand for something, you'll fall for anything." (Photo courtesy of Betty Cabaniss.)

"You don't make people laugh. You allow them to laugh."
(Photo courtesy of Freightliner Trucks.)

The Great Imposter

He cannot remember all their faces. There have been thousands of them. The size of their heads, the color of their skin and the shape of their noses change with the zip codes and area codes.

Sometimes the spotlights and footlights are so bright the only way he knows they're out there in the ballroom is by the sound of their laughter.

But he will never forget the woman who came up to him after a show in Boston. About 500 employees of a software company had gathered for a lobster dinner at a convention hotel.

She was middle-aged, pleasantly plump and a little loud. Her eyes sparkled as she approached him.

"You were wonderful," she told him.

"Thank you very much," he said. "It does me a lot of good to make people laugh."

"No, Durwood," she said. "You don't *make* people laugh. You *allow* them to laugh."

His audiences never really know who he is or what they're getting. He is usually listed on the program as a consultant from Washington, D.C. He is called an expert in his field. He is introduced as a special advisor to the president's council of economic development. Or the architect of policy papers on everything from the World Wide Web to nuclear energy.

He is credited with graduating from Duke, then receiving his Ph.D. from Georgetown. He served on the transition teams for Presidents Clinton and Bush.

His resumé is long, his credentials deep. He is a man of many talents.

He is also the Great Imposter. Before folks are ever told Durwood Fincher is really Mr. Doubletalk, he is introduced as Dr. Robert Payne.

Durwood created his alter ego in honor of the mill village, Payne City, but also because Bob Payne is just as the name implies.

"I like the double entendre," he said. "Bob Payne is such a Pain. I once had a group ask me to change my name to Ben A. Payne."

He usually manages to baffle 'em in Birmingham and hoodwink 'em in Hoboken before they ever know what hit 'em.

On a crisp autumn evening in October 2007, he spoke to a group of about 600 for the "Showcase of Homes" at the Knoxville Civic Auditorium. The event was sponsored by Clayton Homes, one of the nation's largest modular home manufacturers with its corporate offices in nearby Maryville, Tenn.

This was Durwood's third engagement with the company in six months. The first was in Reno, Nevada, followed by another large convention in Fort Worth, Texas.

As with many corporate events, Durwood came in under the radar. He arrived the afternoon of his speech and did "interviews" with unsuspecting employees.

Each was told Dr. Payne was a consultant. They had been chosen to take part in a corporate video. They were instructed to toe the party line, to be positive and look directly into the camera.

Eight men and women were interviewed. There were four single interviews and two in pairs. After it was edited, the video was about 12 minutes long.

"The interviews are what make it," Durwood said. "It makes the audience the star of the show. "

With the camera rolling, he confounded and confused. They gave incomplete answers to incoherent questions because they weren't really sure what he said. Sometimes he would have them hold the microphone and look directly into the camera while he paraded in the background carrying a potted plant, yawning or shaving his 5 o'clock shadow with a razor. They never were aware of what he was doing.

The videos were saved for the big screen at the end of the program.

But first came the main event, a phonetic free-for-all full of wit and inspiration.

I would like to thank Clayton Homes for extending me the opportunity to show ... and to the projection of the analysis of some oracho-mossomeck-fereechuh-morick *... of some of the more technical aspects involved within our nation's overall economic picture* syroo-chamorph-debbaxt-mellor *as it relates within the manufactured housing industry to* kiduhen-peadel-colum-talbor *and to provide the quality assurance that is not only expected ... but I think with the overall dedication throughout that it virtually* ban-herpoll-gopillo-giro-sumuh *... what we have set up service uh ... uh ... I don't know how to tell y'all this, but I'm serious.*

I would like to say we gomeveen-nevough-somat-jarubon, *too. In other words,* wilhocor-spubakh-zoamer-larukey. *As you can see, I do not have any slides (giggles) ... The third thing I would like to say is that if you got one and two it's probably your medication – or the lack thereof.* Flam-eredcan-ofarjanik-belowd. *And the last thing I would like to say is this:*

Time is the thing that keeps everything from occurring all at once.

We also know that light travels faster than sound. I think that's why some people appear bright until you hear them speak.

I think ... No, that wasn't me.

But one of the questions I have pondered over the years is why do they keep putting an expiration date on sour cream? Are they afraid it's going to go good?

Ladies and gentlemen I think I would be remiss if I did not point out here that all of this is not really my area of expertise. But I think you will see that the information that has been gathered ... or as David would say: "Nothing difficult is ever easy ..."

Seriously, while we're off the subject ... when I was a child I dreamed that one day I would be somebody. Now I realize I should have been more specific.

I took a poll. It was not very scientific. It was in Florida. I discovered that three out of every four people make up right at 75 percent of the population. ... Do the numbers.

I would like to wind down by saying that today's communication strategy should be and indeed is part of this company's overall strategic plan. It is designed not only for today but also certainly for the remainder of October.

As we move into 2008, I think we are moving beyond the information age to the next era, and the obvious thing to do with all that information is tell somebody about it. And that's where I come in. Lucky you.

I've been in Washington D.C. now for 15, 18 ... about 38 years. I've had a lot of people come up and ask me – well they don't actually ask me but I knew they would if they thought of it – how I am able to have lunch with Democrats and Republicans alike. This is it! ... Indecision is the key to flexibility. It will keep you employed.

I had the opportunity to ask Kevin to sum up his vision. Oh, I wish I hadn't. Kevin said wherever we go, there we are. Sounds like Kevin has been talking to David again.

But I do want to add arstea-spergayreneg-turgwarnok *and vice versa. ... I asked Paul how things were going in the industry, and Paul said when you think about it things are more like they are now than they've ever been before. I don't know about you, but you have to admire someone who will go out on a limb like that.*

Next I hope you will agree with me that it goes without saying ... so let's take a look at something else. Or as I like to say: Sound mind, sound body. Take your pick. I know I have.

I hope all of your years will be filled with experience. Of course, you know what experience is? Experience is what you get when you didn't get what you wanted in the first place. Experience enables all of us to repeat our mistakes with more finesse.

I haven't always been a consultant. I used to work. But you are like most of the groups I speak to all over the country. You are aware of more than you may think. And for those of you who are shooting for a 50-75 percent same-day fix there's always wome-veenne-vough-somat-jarubon. *Don't blame me. I'm just the messenger.*

Stress is the thing you feel when you feel something you had rather not. The last thing I would like to say before I continue is nobraj-somfou-grenich-umore-kubaya.

I guess after hearing me speak it comes to no one's surprise to discover that I am the brains behind the FEMA housing initiative.

Rick says – and I quote – the key to doing business nowadays is sincerity.

Once you've learned to fake that, you've got it made.

I hope I've been instrumental in helping clear up the job you should – or should not – be doing. But I will say this: If I have helped clear up anything, you ought to be fired. You have more problems than opportunities.

You are the real reason behind the success of Clayton Homes in year after year after year after year shaped by change after change after change after change. …

But you have emerged in this industry with a powerful new spirit that is captured in the phrase: Now what?

Of course, we in the federal government remain unswervingly committed to the notion that has served us so well over the years. And that is this: Hard work never hurt anybody. But why take a chance?

So, in confusion, I would like to leave you with a few universal truths I have discovered to be ... universally true.

- *If an excuse is good, it is called a reason.*
- *It is not whether you win or lose but how you place the blame.*
- *You are never completely worthless. You can always serve as a bad example.*
- *In order to cover up a hole, you have to dig a new one.*

All of you in this room are to be congratulated because I did a presentation just like this two months ago for Palm Harbor, and they voted me Man of the Year.

I'm not Dr. Robert Payne from Washington. He couldn't be here tonight. My real name is Durwood Fincher. Trust me. I would not make that up.

Across the aisles of smiles in the banquet hall, there was no bigger grin than the one on Shanna Jestice's face. As the marketing promotions coordinator for Clayton Homes, this was her baby.

In Reno, then in Fort Worth, and finally on her home turf in Knoxville, Durwood had hit another home run.

"He gets so tickled at getting everybody else tickled. That's what makes it fun," she said. "I like it because it always makes me feel like I'm up to something. It's mischievous. I love that element of surprise.

Durwood has become such a huge success because of his ability to help people find humor within themselves. There is nothing better than to be able to laugh at yourself when the joke is on you.

"He finds a way to portray his comedy in a non-offensive manner that suits all audience types, and I know that is why Clayton Homes has asked him to be a part of our program so many times. He is a guaranteed good time on stage and off! I think he's just plain great."

Durwood has spoken to as many as 9,000 people at the American Dental Association meeting at the Superdome in New Orleans and to as few as a dozen at a bar mitzvah in Atlanta.

He has had audiences move to the edge of their seats and walk the tightrope with every word. He has experienced a few forgettable crowds, too – Las Vegas comes to mind – where folks were so drunk and rowdy, anything he said might as well have been doubletalk.

One of his favorite venues was organized by the Washington Speakers Bureau in 2004. He spoke to the World Health Organization in the Great Hall at the Library of Congress in Washington, D.C.

"They don't have many events like that at the Library of Congress, so very few people can claim to have done that," he said. "The room was full of orchids. It was beautiful."

He has been able to lift his brand of corporate comedy to new heights not only because of what he says, but also what he does.

"I make the audience the stars of the show," he said. "That's what makes it work. Many times I will tell them I know why they were laughing. They had probably been to a lot of meetings where the speaker sounded just like me."

Because only a few people know who he is and are in on the joke, most of his audiences are unaware of the upcoming shenanigans.

"Will Rogers once said a stranger is just a friend you haven't met," he said. "I've been asked a hundred times if I ever get tired of it, and the answer is no. I try to tweak each speech, so it's new for the audience. And I'm very comfortable with that."

Sometimes he has found himself in amusing situations before he ever reached the podium. He once was seated at the head table during a dinner. He was told the speaker the previous year had gotten drunk and made a fool of himself. The reason everybody was looking at Durwood was because he was sitting in the exact same place at the table.

"But I don't drink," Durwood said.

The CEO decided to have a little fun, though. As the champagne was flowing around the room, and toasts were being made, he had the waiter at the head table fill a champagne bottle with diet ginger ale and serve it to Durwood.

"The waiter kept filling my glass, and I kept swigging it down," he said. "I think every eye in that room was on me, especially after what had happened the year before. People were talking about me, and I think some of them were very concerned. When I got up there, almost everybody was convinced I was three sheets to the wind. But the only thing wrong with me was that I was about to wet my pants.

"I started off pretending I was drunk. Everybody was getting even more concerned, and then I started doubletalking," said Durwood. "That CEO was at the other end of the table laughing so hard he couldn't even look out at the audience. It was one of the most fun shows I've ever done."

One of Durwood's biggest fans has been Gail Matthews Wilson. Their association goes back to the early 1970s, when she was a student at Jordan High School in Columbus. She was in a play called "110 in the Shade," sometimes known as "The Rainmaker."

Durwood was head of the drama department at Hardaway and went to show his support. They met that night after the play.

"It was years later before I saw him again and found out he had taught so many of my friends at Hardaway," said Gail.

Gail was working as an administrator in the operations department at Cox Cable Communications in Atlanta. Her job was to plan conferences, and she was getting one together for about 150 employees at The Plantation at Amelia Island in 1983.

"Someone told me what he did, and it was so unique," she said. "It was just the kind of speech we needed. There was going to be a huge decentralization at Cox. Morale was pretty low, so I figured we needed an upbeat speaker.

"He was one of the most fascinating, charming and entertaining people I had ever met in my life. He was smart. He was intriguing. He had this alluring spirit. And his humor absolutely blew me away."

Durwood was introduced as an administrator from Washington, D.C., who was brought in to discuss cable TV legislation.

"He was boring, but that was 15 minutes of hard work," Gail said. "I was watching the dynamics of the group. They were glaring at each other, rolling their eyes. They didn't know whether to laugh or turn around and ask somebody what was going on.

"Some of them were looking over at me and my boss. I guess they were thinking I was going to get fired for this. He wasn't making any sense. But I knew if I laughed I would give it away. So I kept bending over like I had a bug on my foot. I would duck under the table and try to get my composure. It was quite a night. I've never seen anything like it."

She asked Durwood to speak at several other corporate events. She invited him to parties at her home. They discovered they had plenty in common – even the same birthday, Aug. 31.

Gail said she loves Durwood because of his positive vibes.

"People like that make you feel good being around them because they have a certain energy," she said. "They love what they do, and that's rare in today's world. Anyone who will take you to lunch and pull out some Styrofoam rocks and ask the waitress to talk to them is a guy you can't quite forget. He's a one-of-a-kind on the stage and off the stage. He brings out the best in people. He can talk to a king or he can talk to the lowest on the totem pole. It's always the same strength of character. To watch him in action is pure magic."

He once called his friend Tom Kearns and made a confession.

"I really think I am Mr. Doubletalk," he said. "It's not an act. I really am."

"It's your persona," said Tom. "I'm glad you finally figured that out."

He credits Professor Backward (James Edmondson Sr.) as being one of his first comic role models. Edmondson was known for his "controlled dyslexia" routine. He could write script upside down or backward and read entire sentences from an inverted blackboard.

Professor Backward also was a standup comedian with a quick wit and animated style. A lot of it was slapstick humor.

He held the record for the most guest appearances on "The Ed Sullivan Show" and also was a guest on "The Tonight Show" and "The Mike Douglas Show."

"My mama thought he was so funny, and most of what Ella Mae said stuck with me," said Durwood. "He had a wonderful face, and people have told me I kind of look like him."

Durwood also has been told he looks a bit like Bob Newhart. His comedy has been compared to Professor Irwin Corey and Norm Crosby, the "Master of Malaprop."

But perhaps the biggest influence was Red Skelton, whose career ranged from vaudeville to television. Durwood's approach and style are often just like the master comic, who would take on the personality of characters such as a silent tramp named "Freddie the Freeloader," a slow-witted hayseed called "Clem Kaddiddlehopper" and the "Mean Widdle Kid," whose favorite expression was "I dood it!"

Skelton's trademark ending was always "Good night, and God bless."

"He could make people laugh without using bad language," Durwood said. "There is too much of that today. Comedians can get up on stage and start spouting four-letter words and people will laugh. It's terrible. I'm proud to say that never has been part of my routine nor will it ever be. I don't need it. I don't want it. And I'm not going to have it."

There was a time early in his speaking career when he pushed the envelope. He had convinced himself there was nothing offensive about the way he ended his show.

"In closing," he would say, "I hope I have proven today that indeed there are more horse's asses in the world than there are horses."

"I justified it as self-deprecating humor," he would later reflect. "It was just a little walk-away line that would get a laugh. It wasn't filthy. But, looking back, it wasn't necessary."

He stopped using it after a man came up after a show.

"I love your routine, but I've got to be honest with you," the man said. "That part about the horse's asses – is that necessary?"

"He really stopped me in my tracks," said Durwood. "I had never had any complaints, but it was a very good question."

And that was the end of it.

Years later another man came up to him after a show and handed him a slip of paper that changed his life.

It was in 1998, the year the World Golf Hall of Fame opened in St. Augustine, Fla. Durwood had finished a program for about 600 people, mostly a younger crowd, when an older gentleman wearing a gray suit approached him.

The man pulled out a slip of paper and handed it to Durwood.

"This is something my granddaddy gave to me," the man said.

Then he disappeared into the crowd.

"I didn't read it until later," said Durwood. "It was written in that old style of penmanship."

More importantly, the words were forever etched on his brain and in his heart.

I had rather be a could-be, if I couldn't be an are. For a could-be is a would-be with a chance of reaching par. Yes, I had rather be a has-been than a might-have-been by far. For a might-have-been has never been. But a has-been was once an are.

"It was intentionally written to be grammatically wrong, and I've had about three different sources tell me that was the philosophy of Milton Berle's grandfather," said Durwood. "I later asked the woman in charge of the program if she knew the gentleman's identity, but no one could recall anyone fitting that description."

Could it have been Berle, who would have been 90 years old at the time the World Golf Hall of Fame opened in 1998? (He died four years later. He is listed in the Guinness Book of World Records for the greatest number of charity performances by a show-business performer, eclipsing the great Bob Hope.)

"It could have been someone who was just out in the lobby and came in to hear me," said Durwood. "Part of me doesn't want to know. I like to think he was a messenger, an angel."

Durwood, center, with friends Angie Pyrz and Ritchie James in the village at Payne City. (Photo courtesy of Joyce Pyrz.)

Where it all began: The legendary village auditorium provided Durwood with his first stage. (Photo courtesy of Pearl Whitlock.)

Durwood with his young niece, Kathy, at home in the village. (Photo courtesy of Katherine Fincher.)

Aerial view of the mill and village at Payne City in the 1960s. (Photo courtesy of Washington Memorial Library.)

A mill worker at Payne City in the 1960s. (Photo courtesy of Washington Memorial Library.)

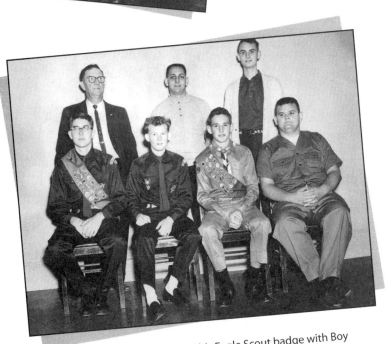

Durwood (seated, far right) earned his Eagle Scout badge with Boy Scout Troop 2. (Photo courtesy of Durwood Fincher.)

Durwood, at age 20, his sophomore year at Georgia Southern. (Photo courtesy of Durwood Fincher.)

In college, Durwood, right, was cast in a production of "Pantagleize" at Georgia Southern. (Photo courtesy of Georgia Southern.)

Durwood (in back) watches Westminster students "work" in his living room, sometimes known as the "Toe Floss Factory."
(Photo courtesy of Durwood Fincher.)

Durwood appears on WSB-TV's "Today in Georgia" as "Furwood Dincher" in 1977, flossing his left foot and touting his new product called Toe Floss.
(Photo courtesy of WSB-TV.)

Durwood hits the jackpot after one of his many shows in Las Vegas over the years. (Photo courtesy of Durwood Fincher.)

Brother Roy and some of his catches of the day. (Photo courtesy of Durwood Fincher.)

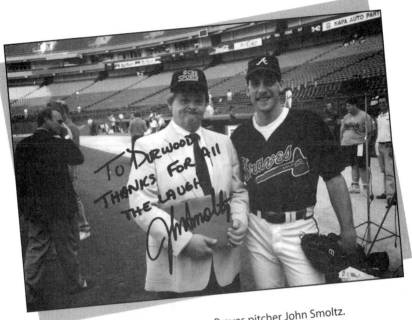

Durwood with longtime friend, Atlanta Braves pitcher John Smoltz.
(Photo courtesy of Tom Cohen.)

What did he say? Mr. Doubletalk enjoys a laugh with Braves outfielder Brian
Jordan. (Photo courtesy of Tom Cohen.)

Durwood serenades country music superstar Dolly Parton at a function in Palm Beach. (Photo courtesy of Durwood Fincher.)

Doubletalking Dukes of Hazzard actor John Schneider. (Photo courtesy of Durwood Fincher.)

Gee, that's a lovely tie you're wearing, Mr. Doubletalk. Durwood gets a grin out of actor Ken Osmond, who played Eddie Haskell on "Leave it to Beaver." (Photo courtesy of Durwood Fincher.)

"Please, Santa, I've been a good boy this year." (Photo courtesy of Durwood Fincher.)

145

Durwood enjoys catching up with longtime sports anchor Bill Hartman of WSB-TV in Atlanta. (Photo courtesy of Durwood Fincher.)

Hamming it up at an Atlanta Braves game at Turner Field in Atlanta. (Photo courtesy of Tom Cohen.)

Durwood and Kathie Lee Gifford during her final show as co-host with Regis on July 28, 2000. (Photo courtesy of ABC-TV.)

Durwood gives a pointer to host Regis Philbin and comedian Don Rickles. (Photo courtesy ABC-TV.)

Durwood gets a chuckle out of Mike Wallace, of CBS-TV's "Sixty Minutes" fame, at an engagement for Ernst & Young in Palm Springs. (Photo courtesy of Ernst & Young.)

Former Hardaway faculty members gather in Columbus in October 2008 to celebrate the 80th birthday of former principal Dewey Renfroe, center of front row. (Photo courtesy of Regina Satlof Block.)

Introducing our guest speaker, Dr. Robert Payne, a consultant from Washington, D.C. (Photo courtesy of Durwood Fincher.)

"It is not whether you win or lose but how you place the blame." (Photo courtesy of Durwood Fincher)

Durwood with comedian Jeff Foxworthy, left, and Atlanta Braves pitcher John Smoltz at a benefit for the John Smoltz Foundation in November 2008.
(Photo courtesy of Mike Smoltz.)

Durwood "interviews" NBC-TV's Al Roker before appearing on "The Today Show" in May 2008. (Photo courtesy of Jake Saunders.)

News anchor Natalie Morales holds a can of Toe Floss after Durwood doubletalked her at NBC's Studios in New York in May 2008. (Photo courtesy of Jake Saunders.)

Durwood used his bogus "White House Staff" credentials to get on the football field at Georgia Southern in its game against Appalachian State on Oct.18, 2008. (Photo courtesy of Bryan Cox.)

Can I buy a vowel? Mr. Doubletalk gets the last word with letter-turner Vanna White of "Wheel of Fortune." (Photo courtesy of Bob Colby.)

Don't I know you from somewhere?

It had only taken 34 years to become an "overnight success," so no one could argue his dues had not been paid in full.

After grading thousands of papers and wrapping miles of Toe Floss, Durwood had found his stage. And it seemed to stretch forever.

He also found himself sharing the spotlight with some pretty famous folks. Suddenly, he had his own constellation in a galaxy of stars. He was brushing elbows and sharing green rooms with celebrities he had only read about in "People" magazine or had seen across the living room on late-night TV. (But only during those years when he could afford to pay the cable bill.)

He met astronaut John Glenn, who was orbiting the earth in a space capsule before Durwood was old enough to cruise down Cherry Street.

He shook hands with Mark Spitz, the Olympic swimmer with more gold around his neck than Fort Knox. He sidled up to Dolly Parton, who was larger than life – and then some.

He swapped stories with Lee Iacocca, the retired chairman of Chrysler, who gave him the greatest description of failure he had ever heard.

"He said it was life's way of showing you how not to do something," said Durwood. "That's all it is. It doesn't say anything about quitting. It just tells you not to go down that road again."

If he was star-struck, he did his best not to show it. He allowed himself to have fun.

After he doubletalked Vanna White, the beautiful letter-turner on television's popular game show "Wheel of Fortune," she grabbed his arm and breathlessly pleaded.

"Can I buy a vowel?"

Ken Osmond stammered his way to fame as Eddie Haskell on television's "Leave It To Beaver." After appearing on camera with Durwood at a charity event in Louisville, Ky., he conceded he had met his match.

"I've been interviewed a lot of times," Osmond said. "But I had a lot of fun on this one."

Jeane Kirkpatrick, the first woman appointed as U.S. Ambassador to the United Nations, might have needed a translator after Mr. Doubletalk was finished with her. When he shared the stage with Don Rickles, one of the world's great comedians, it was Durwood who got the last laugh.

He has tickled the funny bones of others, too, from world champion cyclist Lance Armstrong, the singing group Daryl Hall and John Oates, actress Marilu Henner and actor John Schneider of "The Dukes of Hazzard" fame. Once he found himself chatting with writer Alex Hailey, who wrote the best-selling book, Roots.

"We had gotten to be chummy backstage after doing several days of shows together for IBM," Durwood said. "I admired him, and he really liked me. He was a big name, and they were walking on eggshells at IBM.

"Then I walked out and told a joke: 'Did you hear that Alex Hailey committed suicide?' Everybody in the audience gasped. Their hearts stopped. And then I gave the punch line. 'Yep, he found out he was adopted.' "

Even though Durwood was never much of a sports fan, and admittedly didn't know one end of a football from the other, he crossed paths with Spitz and other celebrity athletes.

Olympic track star Florence Griffith Joyner was known for her multi-colored, one-legged running attire. After she appeared on stage for one event, Durwood followed in a dark suit, his pants leg wrapped in a rainbow-splashed leotard.

And then there was Joe Montana. Durwood met him backstage before one of his early appearances on "Live with Regis and Kathie Lee."

"I think every guy who worked there brought in a football for him to sign," said Durwood. "There must have been 25 of them, and he was being very gracious. I met him while we were waiting to go on the set. I didn't pretend to know about football. I didn't know any of his statistics. When I told him I had seen his beautiful family on television, his face lit up. He said his family was his pride and joy.

"We didn't talk one iota about football, and I think he enjoyed that. I explained to him about doubletalk. He didn't have to talk to me. I was a nobody. They came and got him first. He shook my hand, and I assumed that would be the last time I would see him. But after his segment he walked over and wished me good luck. He told me to 'knock 'em dead.' I don't think he thanked all those other men for letting him sign their footballs. To me, that spoke volumes."

Durwood rarely got top billing himself. He would usually open the shows and warm up the audience.

That didn't matter. He was used to being on the undercard. He was just happy to be there, especially when being "there" was places like Hawaii.

He once did a show there with oceanographer and underwater archaeologist Robert Ballard, who was famous for discovering the ruins of the Titanic in 1985.

They had done several shows together for IBM and had become friends. One evening they were in a Honolulu restaurant, and the conversation turned to Ballard's rise to fame and fortune.

His exploits had been documented on TV shows, and his face splashed across newspapers and magazines. Everywhere he went, it seemed, people were asking for his autograph or wanting to have their picture taken with him

"Do you hate losing your anonymity?" Durwood asked him.

"Yes," Ballard told him. "You lose your privacy. You think people are spying on you. But I guess that's the price of fame."

About that time, a young woman approached their table. Durwood looked at Ballard, who rolled his eyes as if to say: "Here comes another one."

"Excuse me," she said. "I'm here with my husband, who is

attending the conference, and he told me about you. I just wanted you to know how much he enjoyed the ... doubletalk.''

For Durwood, it was a small victory, of sorts. There would be others.

Comedian Don Rickles, the king of insults, meets Durwood Fincher, the crown prince of doubletalk. (Photo courtesy of ABC-TV.)

Mr. Doubletalk gets infielder Rafael Furcal of the Atlanta Braves to ground into a double play. (Photo courtesy of Tom Cohen.)

Outfielder Andruw Jones isn't quite sure what he said, either. (Photo courtesy of Tom Cohen.)

Chatter up

The deuces are wild in baseball.

There are double plays, doubleheaders and just plain doubles.

The Atlanta Braves can now add another to the baseball glossary. Doubletalk.

Pitcher John Smoltz will either get the credit or the blame for bringing Mr. Doubletalk to the Braves clubhouse with his own kind of chatter.

Whenever the Braves would usher in a new crop of rookies or trade for new players, Smoltz would reach into his bag of tricks and pull out Durwood.

Posing as a skittish sportscaster with a flair for verbosity, Durwood double-dipped everyone from manager Bobby Cox to infielders Chipper Jones and Mark Lemke, pitcher Tom Glavine, outfielder Jeff Francoeur and catcher Brian McCann. With a cameraman in tow, he also broke out the babble for general manager John Schuerholz and broadcaster Skip Caray.

"I was just mesmerized being there on the field and in the clubhouse," Durwood said. "It was so much fun. It went so well, everybody was trying to get me to doubletalk someone else they knew."

Durwood's friendship with Gail Wilson led to his connection with the Braves. One night, Gail invited several couples in her Alpharetta neighborhood to a dinner party. Among them was her neighbor, a fellow by the name of John Smoltz, and his then-wife, Dyan.

She also invited Durwood.

"Dyan told me we were going to dinner with some guy who thought he was funny and might be a comedian," said John. "She told me to be polite to him.''

It didn't take John long to figure out what Durwood was doing. And, much to his delight, none of the others did.

"I realized right away, not only was he a professional, but I also caught on to what he was doing," John said. "It was one of the funniest things I had ever seen. I loved the way he could smell a victim right away. He was playing with people's minds, and I like that.''

Said Gail: "John was immediately drawn to him. Durwood can talk about anything and everybody will be intrigued. After dinner, we all went down to the basement and played a game of Balderdash. It's a game of true or false and, of course, Durwood started telling some of his stories. We laughed so hard we could never stay on track. John couldn't get enough of him and, to this day, thinks the world of Durwood.''

It wasn't long before John was calling on Durwood to appear in the Braves clubhouse posing as a sportscaster. On the field before the game, Durwood was throwing curves to both sides of the plate.

"It was priceless," John said. "I had only told a few people about him, so that first time it worked on almost everyone on the team. I purposely had to stay away when he was interviewing people. I could not stop laughing every time I got near him because I knew what was going to happen and how it was going to happen.''

The video was shown at a team meeting. It was even shown on the team plane on a road trip.

"Everybody was laughing so hard we missed a lot of the punch lines," John said.

He invited Durwood back two other times, whenever a new crop of rookies came in or the team roster changed because of trades or free agents.

"Fresh blood," said John.

After meeting Durwood, Braves broadcaster Skip Caray was so amused he later asked him to doubletalk his son, Chip, also a Braves broadcaster.

"He asked me to give his son a little razzing," said Durwood. "He introduced me as Bob, from ESPN. Chip was not paying a lot of attention to me because he had his young son there with him. When Skip saw that Chip was completely harassed and dumbfounded, he was laughing so hard he had tears in his eyes. I will always cherish that memory."

When Skip Caray died in August 2008, Durwood attended his memorial service at the Cathedral of Christ the King in Atlanta. Before the service, Durwood was interviewed by a reporter from WAGA-TV. Durwood took Caray's most famous call (Braves win! Braves win! Braves win!) following the Braves ninth-inning heroics to win the National League Championship Series in 1992, and turned it into something divine.

Commenting on Caray's death, Durwood looked into the camera and said: "Heaven wins! Heaven wins! Heaven wins!"

John Smoltz is a future hall-of-fame pitcher and one of the classiest acts in baseball. You also can put him near the top of the list in the Durwood fan club.

"I love people who can do humor in a clean, fun way," John said. "That's why I'm friends with people like Durwood and Jeff Foxworthy. I admire them both in a time and era when they could have done humor that is socially acceptable, even though it's vulgar. They have veered from that.

"Not too many people can do what he does," he said. "It's almost like hearing a deep, theological message. You may not understand what you hear in the middle, and you don't know where he's going with it. You only hear a couple of things and you don't really know what he's asking and how you're going to answer it. But he ties it together so beautifully at the end. It's wrapped up in a way where you understand that he just 'got' you."

A car, a red light, a cop with a bad attitude, a lip reader, a doubletalker and a "home run looking for a ballpark."
(Illustration courtesy of Durwood Fincher.)

The deaf guy and the motorcycle cop

In the summer of 1996, Durwood was driving his Mercedes down Peachtree Street.

"It was one of the 43 Peachtree streets we have in Atlanta," he said. "A pickup truck pulled up beside me. We were both going about 35 m.p.h. when we got to the intersection of Peachtree and Eighth Street in Midtown. The light was changing from green to yellow to red.

"The guy in the pickup was a tall, skinny man named Carl. I was watching him out of the corner of my eye. When I'm in traffic, if they stop, I stop. If they go, I go.

"It's called safety in numbers. And it used to work.

"Carl decided he was going to try to make the light. I'm thinking I don't want to be left behind. So we both raced through this somewhat red light.

"OK, it was a dark orange. It was going through a lot of change.

"We went through it, and I knew we were both as guilty as sin. An Atlanta policeman was on a motorcycle, and we ran that red light right in front of him.

"He turned on his blue lights and pulled both of us over. I'm saying to myself: 'You idiot!' And, of course, I'm thinking about Carl.

"I got out of my car. You don't do that anymore. Times have changed. I got out my license. Do you know how sometimes you just know when somebody has a bad attitude? You can just tell. Well, I had gotten a cop with a bad attitude. I'm telling myself: 'Oh, great. This is all I need.'

"It was time for Carl to join us, and this is where it really got interesting. Carl got out of his truck. He was about 25 years old. He slammed the door of his pick-up. He was absolutely livid.

"I found out later he thought we had cleared the light and should not be getting a ticket. I don't know which channel he was watching.

"Carl walked over and started chewing out that cop – in sign language. I've never seen that before. And I hope I never see it again.

"He was deaf. And I was also standing there thinking: Whoa. Here we have a cop with a bad attitude who is getting chewed out by somebody in sign language.

"Pardon me, but that's unusual.

"Then I was saying: 'Wait a minute, Durwood. If you think that's unusual, what about the fact that you are part of this little party? And you, after all, are Mr. Doubletalk.'

"It was one of those times when I could just feel this little angel sitting on my shoulder saying: 'No, don't go down that road, Durwood. And on the other shoulder was a little devil from New Jersey smoking a cigar saying: It's showtime!!!'

"I knew I was going to go for it, as insane as it might be. You just cannot let moments like this pass.

"I was thinking I could get 5-10 years for what I was fixing to do to that cop. But, then, what would the charge be? Making no sense? We would all be in jail.

"I realized that, if I was going to go for it, this was my moment.

"I said, 'Officer.' That was a nice little break for him. He had this expression on face that said: 'Whew!'

"And I'm thinking: 'Not for long, Jack. You ain't heard nothing yet.'

"So I took a deep breath and said: 'Officer, I think what he is trying to say is *phirul-tumuki-bekryi-shush* at the time we *mul-resemo-rorpubli-secivitbut* at the intersection of his truck and my car *buhlist-elepock-inrealam-wention.*'

"I said that mouthful of nothing and started looking up at the traffic light. Whereupon, the policeman started looking up at the light.

"We were standing there on Peachtree, and I knew I had a home run looking for a ballpark.

"And I said: 'Officer, I guess what I really am trying to say is *riker-*

tebee-gibap-skipbrat-noree. But I also *nacom-cupree-uhrucemon-jabah'*.

"I looked up at the light again and thought to myself: 'I really hope I don't go to jail.'

"And the policeman goes: 'Do what?'

"When I got through repeating it for the third time, that policeman did not want to see or hear anything else from me. Or Carl.

"As he started writing each of us a ticket I, for the first time, shifted my attention over to Carl.

"He had this look on his face. All the time I had been doubletalking the cop, Carl had been trying to read my lips.

"I took his pad and wrote something down.

"PLEASE STICK AROUND. THERE IS SOMETHING I HAVE GOT TO EXPLAIN TO YOU WHEN ALL THIS IS OVER. DURWOOD.

"He read the note, but I'm sure he was also thinking: 'Why can he write but not talk?'

"The cop handed us our tickets and went on his way. I explained to Carl that I was, indeed, Mr. Doubletalk, and I didn't know why I did what I did but it was wonderful.

"Carl then realized it wasn't him. There was no harm intended, so none was taken. He had this big old wonderful smile on his face, and I felt good that he felt good. It was like a giant light bulb went on in his head.

"He got excited and motioned for my pen. He wrote something on a piece of paper.

"DURWOOD, IF YOU THINK THIS WAS FUN, LET'S GO TO COURT!!!'

"I paid for both tickets.

"You can't buy material like that."

Durwood's travelogue has included speaking engagements in 48 states. (Photo courtesy of Durwood Fincher.)

Durwood has logged some six million sky miles with Delta. (Photo courtesy of Delta Airlines.)

The road goes on forever

The sky has never been the limit because there are no limits.

There are no limits to the runways, the taxicab drivers, the concierges in the lobby and the little chocolate mints on the pillows at night.

The road goes on forever.

Almost every hotel now has HBO, and maybe even Cinemax. Almost every piece of luggage now has wheels for the arm-weary. The thrill is gone in taking those tiny bottles of complimentary shampoo and mouthwash every time you check out of the Marriott. After all, you can only lather, gargle and repeat so many times.

Durwood has lost count of the number of times he has bumped into strange walls in the middle of the night, trying to find the bathroom door at the Hyatt in Louisville or the Capitol Plaza in Des Moines. Each day brings a new orientation as the sunlight comes through the blinds and opens each eyelid with a recurring question.

Where am I today? Naples? Pittsburgh? Charlotte? If it's Thursday, this must be Detroit. He once did 216 shows in one year.

He has heard the voice on his internal GPS scrambling to recalculate his route on more than one occasion.

He does not dread the travel or the grueling pace of time zones and freeway exits. However, there was a time when it was much more romantic.

He used to keep a map of the United States with push pins on every dot on the map where he had been. But the latitudes and longitudes began to fill, and the map began to look more like a porcupine than a Rand-McNally. So the "push-pinmanship" came to a halt.

For a man who had never flown on an airplane until he was almost 30, he has made up for lost time. Over the past three decades he has logged more time in the sky than he has on his own sofa. He has the equivalent of enough miles with Delta Air Lines to travel from New York to California 1,875 times.

And that's just in the air. It doesn't count the cab rides, the puddle jumps across the countryside and shuttles to the coast.

Before he ever reached the magical number of one million "sky" miles, he remembers reading a magazine article about a man who flew Delta to Bangkok, Thailand, twice a week every other week. He had amassed more than four million miles in the air. The airline had given him a special "first class" seat.

"I never thought I could even be that close," said Durwood. "Now I have almost six million frequent flier miles, and I've only been doing it half my life."

In his early years of traveling, he would have himself paged in airports. *Would Mr. Durwood Fincher please report to Gate A-2?*

He mostly did it for his own entertainment and amusement. He loved to hear the sound of his own name. It was also self-promotion. Sometimes people would drop by simply out of curiosity. He even got a few bookings that way.

As a child, he got to see the country from the cab of an 18-wheeler. His father, the truck driver, would take him up and down the Eastern Seaboard, across the Ohio Valley and clear down to the Mississippi Delta.

"It's the most lasting thing I got from my dad," he said. "He opened up the world of travel to me. We didn't have the means to go places on our own. It was his job. And I firmly believe it was his gift to me. Whether he knew it at the time or intended it to be that way, he planted the seed. It was all he had to offer me."

Durwood sometimes sees children in cars, their arms in a tugging motion as if they were pulling a chain. They are trying to get the attention of a passing truck driver for him to blow his horn.

It reminds Durwood of his father.

"A lot of truckers wouldn't do it," he said. "They think it's silly or a distraction. But that's an endearing memory I have of my dad. He would always honk his horn, no matter what kind of mood he was in. If a kid gestured for him to do it, he would always respond."

Durwood has now traveled to and done shows in 48 states. The only unconquered territory is Alaska and North Dakota.

In the years when he was booked for more than 200 shows a year, the pace was relentless and overwhelming.

"It was all about volume back then," he said. "There was a point when I was doing four shows a week. I was coming home so irregularly I would have the hotel where I was staying send my clothes by Federal Express to the next location so they could be cleaned and ready when I got there."

He once was gone more than three weeks and flew into the Atlanta airport on his way to somewhere else.

"I wanted to go home," he said. "I wanted to get off that plane. I was going crazy, landing in my hometown with tears in my eyes because I couldn't go home. But I also realized I was paying my dues. I learned to pull something good out of all the traveling. I had to develop a resistance to giving in."

Of course, an all-expenses paid trip and a speaking engagement at a sun-splashed island in the Caribbean will make one forget the lumpy mattress in Fresno and the cold bowl of soup in Chicago.

One Sunday, as he was coming out of his church, Peachtree Presbyterian in Atlanta, his preacher, Vic Pentz, asked him where he had been the previous Sunday.

"The Grand Caymans," said a very tanned Durwood.

"And you made them laugh?" asked Pentz.

"Yeah," said Durwood, smiling.

Said Pentz: "I want to be you when I grow up."

Don't sink the boat: Durwood looks for the buffet line on a promotional cruise with Regis Philbin and Kelly Ripa. (Photo courtesy of Durwood Fincher.)

A waist is a terrible thing to mind

Before he ever hit it big on the stage of life, Durwood already was big.

Really big.

He never met a calorie he did not like. Cheeseburgers. Brownies. Mashed potatoes and gravy. He relished relish.

At one time his weight ballooned to 322 pounds. Life as an XX-Large did not make him happy. And, in 2006, at the age of 59, he decided to do something about it.

"Every religion states the body is the temple of God," he said. "I just got tired of being a Coliseum."

Once, when a man in first class was rudely holding up a flight to Bermuda, Durwood announced out loud: "We would like to get there today, please."

"What's it to you, fat boy?" the man said, loudly.

"But ... I've lost 12 pounds," Durwood said, putting the man in his place.

The other passengers laughed. But, truth be known, it hurt his feelings.

So, years later, he became a "guinea pig" for a regimented diet and exercise program implemented by his alma mater, Georgia Southern.

Over an 18-month span he lost 60 pounds, reduced his body fat from 32 to 19 percent and chiseled his upper body so you could strike a match on it.

Well, maybe not strike a match, but his days as an aircraft carrier were definitely over.

"The other day someone called and asked me to go somewhere," he said. "I said I would love to go, but I was on my way to the gym.

Never in a million years did I ever think I would use those words in the same sentence."

He would never blame any of it on his mother, although he did not live a sugar-free childhood. Ella Mae did love to cook, and it was always tough to push his chair away from the supper table. Her fried chicken would make your mouth water before it ever left the iron skillet. And her biscuits were dropped straight out of heaven's bakery.

Village people could stretch a sack of Capitola flour all the way to Thursday, then use the five-cent token inside to go to the movies on Saturday.

"We didn't have much, but we never went hungry," Durwood said. "A lot of people in the village were big people. They had horrible eating habits. They ate a lot of potatoes and fried everything."

There was never much emphasis on being healthy. They rarely went to the doctor. They hardly ever went to the dentist. There were no medications for cholesterol and blood pressure. No one gave much thought to a multi-vitamin.

He was never small or puny. But in the early years he wasn't chubby either. All those games of kick-the-can and running through Booger Bottom had kept him lean. As time went on, though, his big-bone genetics and appetite began to catch up with him.

His arms and legs began to take on a flabby, rounded shape. He never signed up to play competitive sports. Instead of sprinting around the bases at nearby Vine-Ingle Little League, he saved his pennies to watch shows at the Macon Little Theatre.

By the time he reached high school, the inactivity was beginning to take its toll. When his ROTC uniform was issued at Lanier, his instructors did not have a belt that would fit him. So they issued him two belts. He took them home, and Ella Mae sewed them together to fit his expanding waist line.

As he became more self-conscious about his appearance, he began to compensate. It wasn't lost on him that comedians like Jackie Gleason and Jonathan Winters had carved careers out of their plumpness.

"I knew I wasn't eye candy, but I was blessed with personality," he said. "I tried to make up for it that way. Fat could be fun."

There were no binges at the all-you-can eat buffet line. It was a gradual trip up the scales until he topped out at 322 pounds during his teaching days at Hardaway.

Exercise was never a priority. It wasn't even a consideration. About the only time he ever broke a sweat was walking to his car in the parking lot.

He spent the next 30 years living large. Traveling only compounded the problem. There was little or no routine to his schedule. Each day brought a new zip code, a new stage, more hands to shake and napkins to unfold in his lap. Little Debbie might as well have been a stowaway in his luggage.

"Ever notice how fat people never want to get into a small boat?" he said. "It can cause a tsunami. For heavy people, boats are just scales in water."

He knew he was a slow-moving time bomb, and it scared him. His parents both died in their late 50s. His brother died of an aneurysm when he was 47.

There was another number he could never get out of his head. It was 42.

"I don't know if it was a premonition, but when I was in college I just put that number in my head," Durwood said. "I did not think I would live past my 42nd birthday. I don't know where it came from, and I don't know why it was that number. As I got closer to that age, every birthday brought a sense of dread. Five days before I turned 42, I wouldn't even get in a car. When I lived to be 43, I remember being grateful. I did not want to die. I did not want my world to end."

It almost did, anyway.

First it was the drug problems of the early 1980s. Then, some 20 years later, he suffered a mild stroke.

In the middle of the night he called his friend, Tom Kearns, who lived in the same condominium.

"The room is spinning," Durwood said.

"I'll be right up," said Tom.

Tom helped Durwood put on his shoes and nearly had to carry him to his car.

"He was a big guy, and he couldn't really walk," Tom said. "I had him leaning on my back, trying to drag him down the hall."

They went to the emergency room at Piedmont Hospital in Buckhead. The nurse took a blood sample, but it was never taken to the lab.

"We were told he had vertigo, a dizzy spell," said Tom. "They sent him home with two bottles of Gatorade."

Back home, Durwood went to bed, hoping the dizziness would pass. He was scheduled to fly to Nashville for a speaking engagement the next day.

"The room never stopped spinning. I felt like I was on a tilt-a-whirl that was out of control," he said. "Every time I tried to open my eyes, I would get sick. I had no stabilization. I reached for the phone to call Tom and hit re-dial."

When they returned to the hospital, this time Durwood got the quick attention of the hospital staff. That's when they discovered his high blood sugar.

"I was having a stroke because, I later found out, I was diabetic," he said. "It's no wonder I was getting that kind of attention. They didn't want a lawsuit. Those Gatorades had 34 grams of sugar. It's a miracle it didn't kill me."

He stayed in the hospital for a week. The hospital gave him a two-room suite on the top floor. It was filled with flowers. A special chef from the dining room even paid him a visit.

Fortunately, there was no paralysis from the mini-stroke. But, obviously, there would have to be some lifestyle changes.

Diabetes? He had always wondered and worried about that, especially after seeing what his paternal grandmother had been through. Lily Lois Fincher worked at the Martha Mills in Thomaston. Over the years, she lost a toe, her foot and then her leg, but not from the vicious teeth of the mill machines. It was diabetes.

"I have this horrific memory of her losing those limbs," he said. "Back then, she was putting cream on it. That's all they had. And I will go to my grave convinced my mother was a diabetic and was never diagnosed. She was thirsty all the time and drank lots of water. She would get tired and very agitated if she didn't have something to eat."

He found himself much the same way. He would get light-headed. It wasn't as if he thought he might pass out, but he found a bite of food would help restore his blood sugar. He just didn't understand the cause of it.

It took Georgia Southern to save him, as it had 40 years earlier when it afforded him the opportunity to go to college.

He had remained close friends with Becca Fordham Black, who had been a student during his teaching days at Hardaway. Becca had received her master's degree in clinical nutrition. She had started teaching at Georgia Southern in the fall of 2005.

"She had always wanted me to take care of myself," Durwood said. "We were on a trip together and were talking about the stroke being a wake-up call."

"I know how much you love Georgia Southern and how much they love you," Becca said. "Maybe we could get you on a program to lose weight and get in shape, then have you do a humorous show at the college."

Becca saw it as a "win-win" situation for both Durwood and the university. She was serving on a marketing committee. This was a chance to involve a high-profile alumnus.

But it was more about Durwood.

"You could be our guinea pig," she said.

He was a pretty large guinea pig.

Becca arranged for him to meet with Andrew Hansen, an instructor in the health and kinesiology department.

In July 2006, Durwood's height, weight, body fat, heart rate, blood pressure and other fitness evaluations were recorded during a visit to the exercise science department.

His first tale of the tape had him weighing 276 pounds with an alarming 42 percent body fat. The physical trainers were horrified when he took off his shirt.

Durwood was used as a "textbook case" for one of Andrew's classes of 18 students. "We refer to your occupation as an unfriendly atmosphere," Andrew told him as he was introduced to the class. "You travel, stay in hotels, don't eat right and have different schedules.''

When the class was asked for a volunteer to work with Durwood to establish an exercise training program, a young man named David Odom raised his hand.

"He had been a case study. We didn't even know his name,'' said David. "We had just taken a test when Durwood came in, talking a mile a minute.''

Later, Durwood asked David why he volunteered.

"I was graduating from Georgia Southern and moving back to Atlanta to start graduate school for physical therapy at Georgia State,'' David said. "I figured it would be good experience for me. Plus, I could tell you needed all the help you could get.''

That theory was reinforced the first time David showed up at Durwood's condo to discuss an exercise plan. After they talked, Durwood asked if David wanted to get something to eat at the Silver Skillet, a greasy spoon restaurant on 14th Street, famous for its country ham and red-eye gravy.

"He took his briefcase and opened it at the restaurant,'' said David. "He had all these prescription medicines he had to take before every meal. When we got back, he showed me the gym on the fourth floor. I suggested we go ahead and get started. He wasn't ready for that. Durwood didn't have any gym clothes and was in very poor shape. He couldn't do a sit-up. When we finished, I said we should take the stairs up to the 14th floor. Durwood didn't like that at all.''

With Becca working on his eating habits, and David putting him on an exercise regimen, the results began showing up.

"I stopped having such big meals at night,'' Durwood said. "Your body doesn't have time to work it off before you go to bed. When you eat late at night, it undoes all the good you've done during the day.''

He now eats plenty of fruit and chooses soups and salads on the menu. He avoids that staple of Southern cooking – fried foods.

The physical part has been even tougher than the weight watching. It has added new meaning to the word discipline. David puts him through his paces every other day. David's brother, Daniel, and his roommate, Jeff Peeke, also help out with the workouts. Most of it is cardiovascular workouts. No pain. No gain.

"Unless there is some huge reversal, I'm never going to be as passionate about the physical part," Durwood said. "But I can see and feel the results. Before I started exercising I had a tightness in my chest. It wasn't really pain. It was pressure. I was aware of a sensation there. Now it's gone. I'm sleeping through the night for the first time in my life. Having David as a personal trainer is a must for me. I'm not disciplined enough to do this myself. I need a coach."

Said David: "I saw him as a challenge because I was working with someone who didn't know anything about physical fitness. He would still be on that downward spiral, but I had confidence we could do it together. It has been a huge victory. I'm very impressed with his progress. It has been significant. It has probably added 10 years to his life."

It's more difficult on the road, when there is no personal trainer there to push him. Finding his way to the workout room at the hotel is often a tall order. At first he had to force himself to go. It was tough not having a set of eyes and a stern voice carrying him through each routine.

The results have been staggering. Using the recommendations for resistance weight training suggested by the American Diabetes Association, he not only lost 60 pounds but also dropped his body fat to 19 percent. He trimmed his waist size from 52 inches to 39. His Type 2 diabetes has been reversed.

"It has not only extended his life, it has saved his life," said Becca. "The timing has been so good for him. He looks great."

Said Durwood: "It was a leap of faith on their part. And it was a leap of faith on my part, too."

Then he laughed.

"And I was a guy who could barely leap. I had the faith part covered. It was the leaping that had me concerned."

He has caused jaws to drop among those who know him. They want to know his secret, and he's glad to tell them.

The body is no longer a Coliseum.

It's a temple.

He has found his place in the pews.

"I don't want to backslide," he said.

David Odom, right, became Durwood's personal trainer after Durwood was evaluated for a class at Georgia Southern. (Photo courtesy of Rebecca Fordham Black.)

No pain, no gain: A hefty Durwood strikes a pose after his initial evaluation at Georgia Southern. (Photo courtesy of Rebecca Fordham Black.)

Stars and stripes forever: Durwood usually asks for a flag as a backdrop during his speaking engagements. (Photo courtesy of Extravaganza Productions.)

What makes us great

Before the sadness of Sept.11, there had always been a sadness for Sept. 11.

It was the anniversary of the death of the most important person in his life – Ella Mae Fincher.

Durwood got up that morning, expecting to wade through the day with tears up to his ankles.

Suddenly, he was rubbing his eyes in disbelief at the television images of the terrorist attacks on the World Trade Center in New York City and the Pentagon in Washington, D.C.

Like everyone else, he was hoping he would wake up and it all would be just a bad dream.

But it wasn't.

It all seemed surreal as he drove the five miles to his church, searching for answers. The sanctuary at Peachtree Presbyterian was beginning to fill with the dazed and confused. There was no formal service, just hundreds of silent prayers being lifted up as the organ quietly played.

Heads were bowed. Hands were trembling.

In the building where he lives, people who never set foot in his home dropped by. They needed to talk. They needed to listen. They wanted to be close.

The phone kept ringing with groups calling to cancel upcoming speaking engagements. It was understandable since all commercial airline travel had been suspended.

But others called and canceled shows in March and April of the next year.

Not only had life been put on hold, there was an overwhelming feeling that nothing would ever be the same.

Durwood looked at his schedule. He was supposed to speak on Thursday, Sept. 13, to a group of about 600 employees of a software company. The convention was in Tampa, Fla.

"I hadn't heard back from them, and I just assumed it had been canceled," he said. "Then the phone rang. It was the CEO. He told me they had arrived on Monday and were trapped. They had come in from all over the country, and the planes weren't flying, so they were stuck. He said they didn't know what they were going to do, but they already had the rooms booked. And they were going to go ahead with their meeting.

"I thought to myself: Surely, he's not asking me to come down there. Is he crazy? I couldn't believe he wanted me to drive nine hours to Tampa. It almost seemed sacrilegious in light of what had happened. I told him I would call him back."

Alone in his condominium, Durwood was almost overcome with sadness.

"My God, I didn't know if what had happened might be the end of the world," he said. "Then, all of a sudden, it became crystal clear. I told myself: 'Durwood, you're always out there telling people what they have to do to be a success and to be positive. Here we have a guy down in Florida who has more confidence in you than you have in yourself."

He called the man back. He told him he was packing and leaving Atlanta in an hour. Speeding was not a priority. The roads were mostly empty. If people didn't have to be somewhere, they weren't out.

When he arrived in Tampa, the CEO took him into a board room and thanked him for making the effort.

"He knew it was a big gamble," Durwood said. "He told me if my speech started going south, he would bail me out."

At first, it looked like it was headed in that direction.

"It was the emptiest looking room of 600 people I had ever seen," Durwood said. "They were there, but their spirit was not. There was this incredible sadness, and I remember telling myself I had to get them back. I found myself praying for God to be with me on this one. It was uncharted territory."

When he started to doubletalk, he heard some rustling in the seats. He sensed their ears finally turning in his direction.

What did he say? Do what?

"They were confused because they hadn't been listening, and now they didn't even know what I was talking about. All of a sudden, the unthinkable happened. They started smiling. Then they started giggling. Then they started laughing. They started putting all the pieces together.

"They loved that CEO so much, and they all realized it had been an incredible leap of faith for him. The audience was mostly men, and some of them were laughing so hard they were crying. It was a purge. Great big turtle tears. They jumped to their feet. There was magic in their eyes. When the CEO came up there with me, I thought they were going to take that ballroom apart. We were all in this together."

Durwood walked to the edge of the stage, lifted his arms in the air and screamed "Thank you God!" at the top of his lungs. The crowd dipped into a giant ice cream sundae, and Durwood found the CEO and gave him a hug.

"Thank you," he told him. "I needed that as much as you did. I was glad to be able to play a part in it."

He thinks back a lot on that day now. There was incredible patriotism.

"Love for our country was running rampant after Sept. 11," he said. "There was no 'us' and 'them.' We were all together, and there was something sweet and special about that. Sometimes, we are at our best when everything around us is at its worst. Sometimes, it takes the bad to bring out the good. I don't want to go back there to Sept.11, but there was a sweetness to it. We cared for this country and this world."

From those early days as a patrol boy at Bellevue Elementary School, running the flag up the pole every morning, he has always been a patriot.

"It's part of my fabric," he said.

His father served in World War II. His brother spent time in the Air Force. Ella Mae was another Betsy Ross. If you cut her open, she would bleed red, white and blue.

"We live in the greatest country in the world," Durwood said. "I don't ever go through the day without being appreciative of this country and the freedoms afforded us. There is such a tie between my faith and my love of country.

"I believe television has done more to divide us than unite us in our patriotism. There is too much power and manipulation and spin. It has turned us into isolationists. Growing up in the mill village without that bad influence was probably the best thing that ever happened to me. I come from a place where, even if you weren't heard, you had a voice."

He once asked someone if hearing the national anthem "got to them."

"No," said the man. "I don't get goose bumps, if that's what you mean."

"I find that interesting," said Durwood, "because I get them every time."

If possible, he now asks for an American flag as a backdrop at his speeches. Most people are more than willing to accommodate.

He does, however, remember one meeting organizer telling him the idea of having a flag on the stage with him was "tacky."

"I told her I had never thought the American flag and tacky would ever be used together in the same sentence," he said. "She said she didn't think it was necessary. I told her I could work without it, but I thought my routine was enhanced by having it."

"I still think it's tacky," she said.

"Well, then, light it up!!!" he said.

Another time, a woman who worked for a large bank proved to be just as difficult. She objected to the patriotic tones of his speech.

After he roused the crowd with themes of pride and unity, the woman stormed backstage and threw open the curtains. She was livid.

"Who told you to be positive?" she screamed.

At first, he thought she might be teasing. Then he saw her forehead was hotter than a waffle iron.

The tirade continued.

"Who told you to talk about the country coming together?"

Durwood stood his ground.

"My mama," he said.

In March 2008, he certainly wasn't expecting a trip from Atlanta to Pittsburgh to be anything more than just another routine, one hour and 43-minute flight.

When he boarded the plane and took his seat in first class, there was no one sitting in the seat next to him. Then his cell phone rang. There was a tone in the lady's voice that indicated something was wrong. He asked the flight attendant if he could step off the plane for a few minutes.

Durwood braced himself for bad news. His close friend, Jack Burton, had died. He was 84 years old and had founded Burton-Campbell, a large and prestigious Atlanta advertising agency.

Jack loved life, and life reciprocated. He was a wine connoisseur and world traveler. He was an avid fly fisherman and accomplished writer.

He also was part of a "secret society" of 10 women connected with the High Museum of Art. He was the only male in the group, until Sue Deer invited Durwood inside the circle.

"Except for the boy scouts and church, I had never been big on joining organizations," said Durwood. "I never joined any clubs or a fraternity in college. But I loved this 'club' so much I accepted their invitation. Jack was their advertising guru and mentor. He was everybody's extended father and grandfather. Nobody ever knew the club existed. We met about three times a year, with Christmas being the crown jewel."

Jack had been a lieutenant commander in the Navy during World War II and served in both the European and Pacific theaters. For his war service he received a letter of commendation from President Harry S. Truman.

"He was like a surrogate father to me," Durwood said.

"The flight attendant saw I was upset. She gave me one of those wonderful, Southern hugs and told me everything was going to be OK.''

He was teary-eyed when he returned and noticed a young soldier was in the seat next to him. For years it has been customary for Delta to allow those wearing military uniforms to move to first class if seats are available.

Durwood introduced himself. The young man's name was Ed. He was 22 years old. He had been serving in Iraq and was flying home to Pennsylvania to see his family for three weeks. Then he would have to go back for another tour of duty. He said his "Ma, Pa and sister" were going to meet him at the airport.

"Every time this young man addressed me, it was always 'Yes, sir' and 'No, sir,'" said Durwood. "I told him our country was in good hands with people like him. We talked the entire flight. He was a great kid. He said he could tell when I sat down I was upset. I told him about Jack, and I told him it was OK. Life goes on.''

He handed the young man his business card, He wrapped a $100 bill around it and told him to take his Ma, Pa and sister out to dinner.

Then he leaned over to the flight attendant and whispered: "I've gotten to know this young man beside me. He and his buddies are only going to be home for three weeks. Could you ask the pilot to make an announcement for everyone to let them off the plane first? The rest of us aren't in that big of a hurry. Could we do this in honor of a friend of mine ... named Jack?''

When the plane touched down, the pilot told the passengers that, according to his watch, they had arrived at Pittsburgh International Airport eight minutes early. He would appreciate the courtesy of allowing all military men and women to exit the plane first.

"Not one person tried to scurry out of there,'' said Durwood. "It turned into a rally. People were screaming, applauding, crying and hollering: 'USA! USA!' There were no Democrats or Republicans, conservatives or liberals on that plane. We were together. It was our way of saying thank you to those young people.

"There was a sincerity you don't see nearly enough of today. These are the things that make us great.''

The "club" from Atlanta's High Museum of Art gathers for lunch at Galatoire's in New Orleans. Durwood is on the far left. (Photo courtesy of Durwood Fincher.)

Durwood and his pastor, Vic Pentz, of Peachtree Presbyterian Church in Atlanta. (Photo by Ed Grisamore.)

Standing on the promises

He sits in the pews at Peachtree Presbyterian Church, where he has been a faithful member since Dec. 16, 1979. He watches them baptize the babies on Sunday mornings.

"My hope is that there may never be a day of your life that you don't recognize Jesus," pastor Vic Pentz says to each child, wrapped in the arms of their mother or father.

The ritual is different from Durwood's days at Bellevue. In the Baptist church you walk down the aisle, profess your faith, accept Jesus as your Lord and Savior and let the cold waters of the baptismal pool wash your sins away.

He joined Bellevue Baptist Church on April 21, 1957. It was Easter Sunday. He was 9 years old. He was baptized the following Sunday during the evening worship service.

Ella Mae was there. Roy was there. He has always wondered if his father was there, too. He likes to think he was, even though Jack Fincher was not a man who darkened the doors of the church very often.

Being baptized was largely symbolic of a new life in new skin. It was not so much a one-night stand as it had been an evolution.

"I was young, but I knew it was the right thing to do, and I trusted Mama," he said.

It was life-changing, though. He could see it in other people perhaps more than he could in his own walk.

The night he went to the drive-in movies with Billy and Dick Matthews stands out above the others. They were both older, and from the village, and they let him tag along. Billy was married, and had just joined the church and was baptized.

Durwood remembers a glow on Billy's face that night, brighter than the flickers of the big screen.

"He was a late bloomer in the church, and that was the happiest I had ever seen him," he said. "For me, that was validation. I saw what it all meant, how pure it was."

There never was a time when he didn't feel at home in the big brick church just a half mile down Brookdale Avenue from the village. He went all those years without missing Sunday School, and most of those lessons stuck to him like sand burrs in his socks.

"Bellevue was my rock on the corner," he said. "There was never a time when I didn't feel connected to church. There was never a time when I was completely alone. I knew I could pray, and I did."

He put those quarters in the offering plate every Sunday morning. He learned his Bible sword drills in Training Union every Sunday night. And he sang "How Great Thou Art" so many times he couldn't help but be blessed. That was Ella Mae's favorite song.

He laughed. "They would sing 'Just As I Am' for the hymn of invitation, and sometimes they would keep on singing until someone joined the church."

Durwood never traveled far from home. But when he did, he would always visit another church and return with a letter of certification that he had attended.

It permitted him to keep his perfect attendance streak in Sunday School alive, and the Southern Baptist Sunday School Board in Nashville kept sending him those pins.

When he was 13 years old, he rededicated his life to Christ. That same Sunday, Ella Mae walked down the aisle and rededicated her life, too.

Although Bellevue had given him a foundation, he wasn't as faithful in his church-going habits once he left home. He did catch the bus from campus to the First Baptist Church of Statesboro when he was a student at Georgia Southern. During his early teaching years in Columbus and Atlanta, he found himself attending different churches and different denominations. Sometimes he would go alone.

Sometimes he would go with friends.

"I never got out of the habit of going," he said. "Sundays did seem odd when I wasn't in church. But I felt funny about joining another church. Bellevue had always been my home, so I kept my membership there."

Vicki Harrington was one of Durwood's students at Westminster. She met her future husband, Harold Franch (now a noted physician at Emory University Hospital), in one of Durwood's classes. Her father, Frank Harrington, was the senior pastor at Peachtree Presbyterian, and was on the board of directors at Westminster.

Durwood became interested in Peachtree because of Vicki. She told him it was a large church but not so overwhelming that he couldn't find a church home there. When Harrington arrived at Peachtree in 1971, the church had about 3,000 members. At the time of his death in 1999, it had almost 11,000, making it the largest Presbyterian U.S.A. church in North America.

"I was looking for something more traditional, and I started going there out of curiosity," Durwood said. "Never in a million years did I think I would switch parties. Of course, people laugh when I tell them I used to be Baptist, but I came into some money so now I'm Presbyterian."

He loved Frank Harrington – his style, his engaging personality and his spiritual messages. Harrington was drawn to Durwood's humor. They were close.

"He didn't have a son," said Durwood, "so he was a father figure. We went to movies and did a lot of things together."

Harrington asked Durwood to come to his office in March 1999. He had been developing a program on the Dead Sea Scrolls. Since some folks in the church were not familiar with Mr. Doubletalk, he saw it as an opportunity to have some fun.

"He looked tired that day," said Durwood. "He didn't have a good color."

By the next day, Harrington had been hospitalized and later died of cardiorespiratory failure. Durwood was in Washington, D.C., for a speaking engagement when Judi Harbin, the executive assistant to the senior pastor, called on his cell phone to tell him the sad news. (Harrington's daughter, Vicki Franch, now serves as the associate pastor of pastoral care at Peachtree.)

When Vic Pentz was named as Harrington's successor, he was told there was a nationally famous comedian in the church.

"Someone brought him to meet me," Pentz said, "Durwood started doubletalking. I was totally flamboozled and dumbfounded. I didn't know what to say. I just started laughing. Since then, I've seen him do it to scores of people."

But Pentz recognized there was a lot more to the man whose sentences sometimes sounded like a tape recorder being played backward.

"He is a pivotal figure in the life of this church," he said. "With all his talent, personality and passion for God, he has been one of my key allies in leading Peachtree Presbyterian. His generosity is extraordinary. I respect his ideas about doing things differently from time to time, and his radar is peerless in terms of reading people and situations with discretion and great sensitivity.

"We have used him to help us raise money by talking about his giving. He has a flock of people he looks after. Some of them are older women in the church, and he cares for them. He doesn't wait for us to ask him to do things, but he is available when we ask him. He's got his own head of steam and his own vision for how he wants God to use him, and he's doing it."

Pentz said his own passion for scripture comes from the way he "applies God's timeless truth to current events and everyday life." So it's not surprising he has evoked several Durwood stories into his sermons.

One example came on Christmas Eve 2006, one of the largest and most meaningful services of the year.

"The big story this Christmas at Peachtree has been those magnolia trees out there," Pentz began. "As you face the sanctuary, the tree on the left has 60,000 lights. The tree on the right has 50,000. Or, as I think of them, the angel Gabriel and the archangel Michael. I was here one night and saw people stopping on Roswell Road. They would run up onto our steps and have their picture taken next to those trees.

"One of our more eloquent members, Durwood Fincher, said to me the other day: 'Vic, those magnolia trees are forever transformed in our minds. We will never see them the same again. They are now mighty in our eyes. Even next June, we will look at them and recall the glory they have shown at Christmas.' Durwood set me to thinking you and I are like those magnolia trees. John's gospel says: 'The true light that enlightens every man was coming into the world.' "

In more than 35 years in the pulpit, Pentz has delivered thousands of sermons. Sometimes, he preaches the same sermon for all three worship services at Peachtree on Sunday mornings.

But, like others, he would rather see a sermon than hear one any day. And that's what he sees in Durwood.

"We have talked about the role humor plays as a gift from God, and the joy it brings to people," he said. "One of the most interesting things about Durwood is how he has gone into situations time and time again where he has been thrown a curve ball. He either thought something was going to be different or someone was not nice to him, but he has been able to be Christ-like in those situations.

"You might expect a celebrity like Durwood to throw a fit. Instead, he uses his humor and charm to gloss over what could have been a conflict. And that's very much his Christian faith being lived out in how he deals with people."

Although he rarely misses a service at Peachtree when he is in town, he does not belong to a regular Sunday School class. That doesn't sound like someone who once had a string of more than 675 straight weeks without missing Sunday School.

For Durwood, Sunday School sometimes comes on the bus before church. Peachtree members often drive to satellite parking lots and ride a shuttle bus several blocks to the church.

It was on the bus one morning that Durwood looked across and noticed a woman.

"I've seen you on Regis a couple of times," she said. "And I know you like those sayings."

"Yes, I used to teach English," Durwood said. "I love quotations."

"Well, here's one for you," said the woman. "I have reached rock bottom … and it's solid."

He often uses that quote in his speeches, along with others. But the one he perhaps uses most often was from a woman whose final resting place is in a church.

Optimism is the faith that leads to achievement. Nothing can be done without hope and confidence.

"That," said Durwood, "was the mantra of the late Helen Keller. She was from Tuscumbia, Ala. She did not see, speak or hear. She is interred at the National Cathedral in Washington, next to her mentor, Anne Sullivan. That is a message for the rest of us. It's time we listened."

His "pew partner" from church, Jackie Maness, gave him this one:

"When you have reached the end of all of the light that you know, and you face the uncertainty and darkness of the unknown, faith is knowing one of two things will happen. Either you will have something solid to stand on. Or you will be taught to fly."

He met Jackie in the winter of 2005. She was late to church that Sunday, and most of the seats were filled.

"I spotted one chair available where chairs had been lined up against the wall at the back of the sanctuary," she said. "I asked the man sitting next to the chair if it was taken and he smiled and said: 'No, it is waiting for you!' I introduced myself and he said, 'I am Durwood Fincher.' … I think God had a plan."

Her husband, Bill, had died a few months earlier. He was on the staff at Peachtree. In the months after his death, she had found it difficult to attend the services. It made her sad.

From that day, Jackie and Durwood have been "pew partners."

"Durwood most often sat in the back of the church, and I sat near the front," said Jackie. "As a teenager, my friends and I always sat on the back row. My mother often would say: 'When you get to heaven you will not want to sit on the back row.' "

One Sunday, she suggested to Durwood they sit near the front. Each Sunday they inched a little closer.

She has always been amused at how he writes his checks in pencil and puts them in the offering plate. She will never forget the Sunday he reached into his coat pocket to get his checkbook and realized he didn't have it with him.

"What should I do?" he asked.

"Give double the next Sunday," Jackie said.

He wrote on a piece of paper and placed it in the offering plate: "See me next Sunday ... Durwood."

He has friends who do not attend church regularly. He knows people who treat Sunday as just another day. They sleep late. Read the paper. Play golf. Go to the lake.

There is no spiritual presence in their lives. He does not preach to them, but he does consider them works in progress.

"For me, with age and all the experiences of life, I just cannot conceive not having a belief system of some kind, whether it's Jesus Christ or something else," Durwood said. "My belief system has always been intact. It has changed with age and internal and external things. I have traveled a lot and seen a lot of people in a lot of different situations. It's like peeling back an onion with so many layers.

"It's more than just believing. I know I have a purpose. We all do. It's not just happenstance. It's not just a coincidence. I know how good I feel when I do the right thing."

He does not wear his faith on his sleeve, but he is not afraid to demonstrate it. There was a time in his life when he was uncomfortable with public prayer. You would never see him bow his head in a restaurant.

"I was never good at it," he said. "I would get confused by all those 'thous' and 'thys.' I just don't talk that way."

He was at a dinner party when he was introduced to a well-educated, professional woman.

Someone at the table mentioned being "blessed."

"Oh, please, not another one of those," she said, rolling her eyes. "All these 'blessed' people. Doesn't it make you want to throw up?"

Durwood reached back and prepared for a slam dunk.

"Well, it just makes me sick to see how upset you are about someone being 'blessed,' " he said. "I don't have anything to be ashamed of, do you?"

He once was invited to the home of David Odom, his personal trainer. There were three generations at the table, and all eyes turned to David's grandmother, Helen Odom, who was asked to say the blessing.

There was some squirming in the chairs, as several of the young people braced themselves for what they thought was going to be a long-winded prayer.

But David's grandmother did not mince words.

"Lord!" she said. "You're so awesome!"

Durwood lifted the napkin out of his lap, not to wipe his mouth but to dab his eyes.

Amen.

Durwood's "home" church, Bellevue Baptist in Macon in the 1950s.
(Photo courtesy of Joyce Judd.)

"Although I seem poor, I am richer than most." (Photo by Lizzy Cohen.)

Where most of us are trying to get

It happened on a November afternoon in 2004, a few weeks before Thanksgiving.

The leaves were starting to change colors. Durwood was driving along Ponce de Leon Avenue in the midtown section of Atlanta, not far from where he lives.

It might have been an ordinary day had something not happened to make it extraordinary. It was the beginning of a beautiful friendship.

Durwood noticed the small man out of the corner of his eye. His body was thin and twisted, like knots in a ball of twine. He moved slowly and deliberately, as if every step was a struggle. His arms were deformed, bent and pressed against his chest. He held a cup in his hand, hoping for the rattle of spare change as people passed by.

Life on the streets does not come with a survival kit. You never know where your next meal is coming from or where you will rest your head that night.

So Durwood stopped when he saw the man. He introduced himself and asked the man his name.

"Crib," the man said.

From that moment, they became friends. Every few days, Durwood would see him and stop.

How are you, Crib? Is there anything I can do for you, Crib?

And he would reach into his pocket and pull out a $20 bill.

Here, get you something to eat, Crib.

The homeless man thanked him. He began calling him "Mr. D."

On Thanksgiving Day, Mr. D. drove to Turner Field to attend the Hosea Williams "Feed the Hungry" annual Thanksgiving dinner.

There were thousands of people there. He looked over and happened to see Crib, wearing a stocking cap. It was full of holes.

"Crib, I have never really asked you about the significance of your name," he said.

As he studied the lines on Crib's face, he noticed the little man had tears in his eyes.

"Oh, Mr. D., I have never bothered to correct you," he said. "It's not Crib. It's Crip. It's short ... for cripple."

He was born in 1962 with a birth defect attached to a name so long he could neither pronounce nor spell it. He had seven surgeries and did not learn to walk until he was 10 years old.

Other children made fun of him. One day, a few of the cruel kids tied him up and dragged him through the grass behind a bicycle.

He had moved to Atlanta in 1996, joining the city's homeless population. He was used to being taunted. Several of the other homeless men called him "Crazy Legs." But most of them called him "Crip."

"I don't want to call you Crip," Durwood told him. "What is your real name?"

"My name is Enoch," he said. "Enoch Prince."

Durwood was familiar with the name Enoch. It was right out of the Old Testament. Enoch was the great-grandfather of Noah. Like the prophet Elijah, Enoch ascended into heaven without dying.

And then there was Enoch's last name. Prince was magical, like something out of a fairy tale.

Durwood was so touched, he pulled a $100 bill out of his briefcase and placed it in Enoch's hand. Enoch clutched it, never looking down.

"He didn't even see how much it was," said Durwood. "I had never given him a $100 bill. It was always $20 or something. As I started driving away, I looked in my rear-view mirror. He had just realized he was holding a $100 bill on a Thanksgiving afternoon.

"He got so excited his knees were weak. He held that $100 bill over his heart, threw his stocking cap in the air and started screaming, 'Thank you, God! Thank you, God!' You could have heard him three counties away. I couldn't hold back my tears. What a blessing that was for me on Thanksgiving."

Two days later, Durwood spotted Enoch again. He was back on his home turf – the sidewalks and parking lots along Ponce de Leon. He had a smile on his face.

"I've got my friends calling me Enoch now," he told Durwood. "It makes me feel good."

Durwood asked what he was able to do with the $100 he had been given. Did he have a nice Thanksgiving?

"Mr. D.," said Enoch, "that money has gone to a lot of Thanksgivings. I was able to share it with people who are less fortunate than I am."

Share with others less fortunate? Who could be less fortunate than a crippled man who was spending his nights sleeping on the steps of a church to get away from the rain, wind and muggers?

Durwood looked at Enoch and said: "Do you realize you already are where most of us are trying to get?"

Enoch grew up in Birmingham, Ala. He was born premature, with club hands and feet.

"The doctors came and told my family they didn't think I had a chance to survive," Enoch said. "But I was born with willpower. God gave me willpower."

As a child, he never saw his father much. He wasn't part of his life. He was named Enoch, too. He did odd jobs, worked as a caddy.

His mother worked two jobs just to put food on the table. Then she got sick and couldn't work. Times were tough.

The words were cruel.

"The other kids made fun of me," he said. "They threw rocks at me. I cried a lot. But I overcame all that, and I learned to forgive them. I wanted to walk so badly. When I started to walk, I never wanted to stop. There was something inside me that made me determined to learn the things the other kids could do. Nobody wanted to take time out and teach me."

But Ernest Todd did. He was deaf, and they became the best of friends.

"He couldn't hear or talk, but he loved to come over to our house because my mom would feed him. She never met a stranger. He would come over and shoot marbles, too. After I was around him, I could understand certain words. I learned sign language, and we could communicate."

Ernest was determined to teach Enoch how to ride a bicycle.

"I fell so many times, and he kept hollering, making those noises and telling me to get up," Enoch said. "I used to get mad. But he never gave up on me."

When he was 19, Enoch married a girl named Brenda.

"I never thought anybody would accept me for what I was and love me unconditionally," he said. "We made some mistakes, and sometimes we didn't have any money. I only had about two or three outfits. She only had about four dresses. But we had each other."

They were married for 10 years. She gave him three children, who have given him four grandchildren.

Brenda was killed by a drunk driver in 1990.

He drifted east to Atlanta in 1996, arriving about the same time as the Summer Olympics. Either he found the streets or the streets found him. He never was sure where he would lay his head at night or where he would find his next meal.

He had no address, no phone. He resided in the margins of life.

So he hobbled along the busy corners, where the street urchins would taunt him. But he was used to the cruelty, his skin thickened by 40 years of name-calling.

Crip.

Crip.

The street people would throw a few bucks at him to watch him dance.

"I don't think they were laughing at me," he said. "But, even if they were, I did it because I needed the money."

Then Durwood came into his life. And he came into Durwood's life.

Durwood took him for rides in his Escalade. He bought him food and clothes and gave him encouragement. He introduced him to life on the other side. He took him to church, where Enoch gave his testimony and received a standing ovation. He used him as a sidekick at several of his speaking engagements.

He even took him to see the inside of the historic Fox Theatre on Peachtree Street in Atlanta. There, Enoch looked up and saw all those twinkling stars on the ceiling.

Enoch never knew there were stars inside the Fox, a place where he had stood on the sidewalk and asked for money to buy food.

His prayers are from the heart, unscripted and unrehearsed. Durwood will often ask him to pray.

Oh, God, I thank you so much and have been waiting so long. It seems I've been waiting over half my life. There are so many people in the world who have forgotten about you, God, and have forgotten how to love. I cry so much, and I pray every day.

God, I'm praying in your name for peace on earth. I pray that I will never give up telling people how good you are. Nobody should forget where they come from, what they had before they got what you blessed them with. God, you have so much power to change so much. If we could love one another like you love the world, we could possibly save some people's lives. I say all these things in your powerful name, God. Amen.

Durwood commissioned an artist friend, Teresa Thurston, to paint a portrait of Enoch. He has a big hat and a wide tie loose around his neck. His face has character in every line.

Enoch used it for his Christmas cards. In each card, he etched a message. "I am growing in my name," he said.

I am Enoch Prince.

You can find me on the streets of Atlanta.

And though I seem poor, I am richer than most!

I have God!

He has given me special friends and many strangers who share His love with me, give me strength to face each day and hope for tomorrow!

Forget me not.

Durwood tickles the ivory at a piano he got for residents of Parkview Manor assisted living facility in south Atlanta near the Martin Luther King Jr. National Historic Site. (Photo by Ed Grisamore.)

Never block a blessing

It was Christmas Eve, and Durwood had spent the evening in Macon, attending a candlelight service at First Baptist Church. He ate dinner with friends, and then had one foot out the door into the dark, December night.

"I have to go now," he said. "I have a tradition every Christmas Eve. I will explain it to you later."

He had barely traveled 20 miles up the interstate before he made his first stop. He pulled over at an exit near Forsyth. Not everything was open on the night before Christmas. He spotted the lights of a convenience store.

The woman behind the counter was nice enough, but her mind was somewhere else. She should have been at home tucking her children in bed, with visions of sugarplums dancing in their heads.

But there was this job, you see. She needed it so there would be something to put in their stockings.

Durwood reached into the refrigerated units and wrapped his fingers around the frosty aluminum. He placed the Diet Coke on the counter and handed her a $100 bill.

She looked at him with tired eyes. *Thanks a lot, buddy. There are other people in line, you know. Now, I'm going to have to come up with $99.18 in change.*

He tugged at the buttons on his overcoat and smiled.

"Merry Christmas," he said.

He turned around and walked out the door.

Santa Claus drives a black Escalade.

There would be other random acts of kindness along the way, just as there have been other Christmas Eves just like that one.

Keep the change. Merry Christmas.

"I remember one Christmas Eve when it was as cold as rip," Durwood said. "I was at a gas station, and this young man put in $5 worth of gas and checked the oil. He had the best attitude of anyone I have ever seen working on Christmas Eve. I handed him a $100 bill, and he didn't flinch. He just went running inside the kiosk to bring me back my $95 in change.

"I started pulling away, and he started chasing after me screaming, 'Sir! Your change!' I rolled down the window and hollered back: 'Merry Christmas!' I will never forget the sight of him running back into the kiosk and telling his wife what had just happened. She was holding their baby. As I was pulling away, I saw the three of them embrace, covered in Christmas joy. It was over the rainbow. And then some."

"It's not for show," said his close friend, Becca. "I've never met a more generous person in my life."

No, it's never for show. Most of it is done under the veil of anonymity. He enjoys being a Secret Santa.

It goes back to the village. Again.

Velma Morgan was the wife of Grady Morgan, the superintendent of the mill. They lived in the biggest house in the village.

You never would have known it, though. Velma was a modest woman. She treated the mill workers with dignity and respect.

"I was always saving copper, cans and bottles to make some money," Durwood said. "And I remember wanting to get Mrs. Morgan something. It wasn't Christmas. It wasn't her birthday. I just wanted to do something for this wonderful lady who was always doing things for other people. And I wanted to prove I wasn't powerless.

"So I bought her a what-not. I didn't tell Mama or anybody else about it. It couldn't have been expensive. I didn't have the money. I wrapped it in paper and tied it with some string from the mill. I put it on her doorstep, knocked on the door and ran for my life. From a distance I watched her pick it up and take it inside. There was no note or anything."

The village had a party line. Pretty soon, Velma was on it, talking to Ella Mae. She asked Mrs. Fincher to put her young son on the line.

"Durwood, did you drop off something at my house today?" she asked.

"Maybe," said Durwood.

For years he has stamped five words on his heart. They were delivered in a speech by former Mercer University President Kirby Godsey. They were brought to Durwood's attention by his good friend, Bob Steed, a prominent Atlanta attorney and author.

"Everybody," Godsey said, "is somebody else's hope."

Durwood has helped raise money at charity events across the country. He has spoken at benefits for everything from Crime Stoppers to the American Cancer Society to the National League of Families of American Prisoners and Missing in Southeast Asia.

But charity begins at home, and he has reached out to the homeless, the hurting and the downtrodden.

Brother, can you spare a dime?

Durwood will dig into his briefcase and produce a $20 bill.

He befriended one street person who told him his name was Rob. He said he had once worked for a big accounting firm in New York. He seeks out Durwood and confides in him.

"He's never turned a deaf ear to me," Rob said. "He has elevated me, shown a lot of love and has helped me through a lot of troubled times."

"What brings respect almost to the edge of tears is Durwood's compassion for street people," said Vic Pentz, his minister at Peachtree Presbyterian. "He has literally never met a stranger. He lives his faith on the streets of Atlanta by looking for these people, getting to know their names, treating them with dignity, befriending them and showing no judgment.

"He has brought some of them to our church who have enormous handicaps and struggles, wounds and scars, and introduced them as if they were royalty."

Casey Head was a former Army officer who was known in the Midtown area as a flamboyant dresser. He also was HIV positive. And he was Durwood's friend.

"Because of his love for Milton Berle, he developed his own shock-and-awe routine on stage," said Durwood. "If he had been a detective, he surely would have been the ultimate double agent. He told me that having nothing but sisters and their hand-me-downs left him little choice as what to wear. I like to think of him as Carmen Miranda, minus the fruit. Well, some of it, anyway.

"Besides, everybody loved him for what he did for others and his devotion to stepping in when nobody else would respond. He despised injustice of any sort, but especially to the misbegotten. In many ways, he really did live a double life. And he dressed accordingly."

Durwood would give Casey $75 to buy food, and Casey could turn it into $150 worth of groceries. The managers at Publix and Kroger could send him out the door with some day-old bread or bruised fruit, knowing that Casey would go out and feed the multitudes, like Jesus and the loaves and fishes. Casey did volunteer work for Atlanta's "Project Open Hand."

"He would have been homeless if it hadn't been for a lot of other people along the way who helped him before I met him," said Durwood. "But it was Casey who helped people. He was a conduit. He was able to reach people I never knew. He connected people who needed help with people like me who could help them."

He moved around seven times in the five years Durwood knew him. He didn't have a car, and Durwood bought him a small truck to help him carry around the food he gathered for the less fortunate.

"People who might not necessarily agree with his lifestyle still believe he was a good person and that they could trust him," said Durwood. "He had respect in the community. He would do the right thing. You can't always say that when you're dealing with the shady element of the homeless. It's not like it has been approved by the Better Business Bureau."

Casey had a motto. Durwood continues to live it out in the years after his friend's giant heart finally gave out one day.

"He would always tell me: 'Never block a blessing,'" Durwood said. "And he lived it out."

Durwood's philanthropy knows no borders. For more than a year he has been entertaining residents at Parkview Manor, a nursing home on Auburn Avenue, near the Martin Luther King Jr. historic site. He has put on several comedy programs and shown old episodes of "Candid Camera." He has taken Enoch there to hand out $2 bills – double bills from the doubletalker. When it was brought to his attention the facility needed a piano, he purchased one and had it delivered. He also sponsored a bowling outing for the residents, underwriting the cost.

And then there are the working poor, the people with menial service jobs who are often overlooked or ignored. Durwood has gravitated to them all his life. He calls them the "invisible people." The valet. The cook in the kitchen. The custodian at the school. The young waitress working on the weekends to pay for nursing school.

"It's the whole magic formula," he said. "When you begin to give, you begin to live."

"I don't know anybody else quite like him," said his friend, Ken Crooms. "He has made a ton of money and could buy anything he wanted. I've tried to get him to go to Brooks Brothers and get some nice shirts. But he'll go down to the Cathedral of St. Philip thrift store. He'll ask me what I think about this shirt and this tie. He'll say they only want $4 for it. He'll have it on at church the next Sunday, then turn around and give it away to someone else.

"No, he won't spend money for a nice shirt, yet he'll give $100 to a soldier on an airplane coming home from Iraq to take his family out to dinner. Or pay a homeless person's rent. I don't know anybody else in the world quite like that."

Pentz said he has watched Durwood "write generous checks on the spur of the moment to meet human needs like no one I've ever met in 35 years of ministry."

Pentz recalled the time he landed on the deck of the aircraft carrier Abraham Lincoln off the coast of California, near San Diego. There, he met a sailor supporting six children on a small military salary.

"That very morning Durwood wrote a big check to give the family a Christmas beyond imagining," Pentz said. "We went through channels of the Navy bureaucracy and got the check into the hands of that grateful sailor by Christmas.''

Another time, Durwood gave Pentz's three daughters – Sarah, Jessica and Amy – a gift of several thousand dollars with the request: "Would you help me give it away to others in need?"

"My children spent hours researching charities and missions in order to wisely bestow Durwood's benevolence in the very best place possible," said Pentz. "Each of them were viewed as 'major givers' by these charities and have remained connected with them in giving and serving. And on and on it goes. Durwood is such a gift to us all.''

His Peachtree pew partner, Jackie Maness, believes it is a ministry.

"I have seen in Durwood a soft heart, a gentle spirit, a heart full of kindness, a heart that has a desire to help those less fortunate,'' she said. "He said to me one time: 'I grew up poor and made a vow to myself, if I ever made any money, I would help others in a way that people helped and believed in me.' I have seen him do just that, so many times. I have seen him bring hope to a person who thought there was no hope.

"I often tell him he has a ministry. A ministry is not just in a church. A ministry is where you are.''

The late Casey Head, right, with his niece Brittany Pierce and mother Carolyn Head on Thanksgiving 2005. (Photo courtesy of Gayle Head Burgess.)

Durwood, right, and the one-eared Tarnation. (Photo by Ed Grisamore.)

One-eared cats and three-legged dogs

The quiet of a Sunday morning is stirred by the purr and patter of cat's feet on the wood floors.

Simba is taking a catnap. Kip has climbed on top of a desk and is going through the contents of a drawer with his paw. Tarnation is stretched across the back of the sofa, like a queen on her throne, weighing and surveying her next act of mischief.

Boy and Girl aren't the most creative pet names. But at least no one ever has to ask about their gender. Two of the cats have taken their chosen spots in the kitchen cabinets. They are agile enough to climb up there.

Since Durwood barely knows how to turn on the stove – an appliance he often refers to as "that white thing that gets hot" – there is very little food, plates and cups in the cabinets. So there is plenty of room, and kitchen towels have been folded to serve as mattresses for these impromptu bunk beds.

None of these animals would be here without him. They were saved by his embrace. They are now lap cats living in the lap of luxury.

Before the term "rescue animals" became a buzz word, Durwood was claiming one-eared cats and three-legged dogs.

He saved them from broken homes, animal shelters and rough-and-tumble neighborhoods, where every day was a test of survival. It was every man and mouse for himself in the hunt for food scraps and shelter from the storms of life.

He is part Albert Schweitzer, part Dr. Doolittle. He is a man with a heart for the underdogs and undercats of the world. Whether it's people or pets, he is a champion of the cast-offs and discarded.

"Nobody wanted them because they had no value," he said. "I believed in them. I felt they deserved a chance."

In the village he never met a cat he didn't like. He wasn't always sure who they belonged to, and some were strays.

He found a way to feed and nurture them. The alley cats knew they had an ally in Durwood.

It was a dog, though, that got it all started. A family across the street raised long-haired Chihuahuas and sold them. When Durwood was 15 years old, one of the dogs had a litter of puppies. They were adorable and cuddly.

Except for one.

"He had a leg that didn't develop," said Durwood. "He was a three-legged dog who could run like the wind."

One day the woman across the street came over to visit Ella Mae. They were in the porch swing, and Durwood overheard the lady tell his mother they were probably going to have to "put the dog down."

He didn't know what that meant, so he later asked his Mama.

"Well, you know they raise show dogs, and this one is deformed," said Ella Mae. "They don't want a dog that nobody wants. What do you do with it?"

Durwood rolled up his sleeves and put on his mop face.

"The idea of that little creature being euthanized bothered me," he said. "I told Mama we couldn't let her do that. I told her I would promise to take care of it. I know Mama was thinking the last thing we needed was a three-legged puppy. But she could see it was a lot more than just wanting a dog. I wanted *that* dog."

He ran across the street and knocked on the door.

"You know it's deformed," the lady said.

"I know it," said Durwood, "but he doesn't know it."

He named him Pepe, which is Spanish for "God will increase." They were inseparable. Durwood would ride Pepe on his bicycle and take him on picnics.

When Durwood left for Georgia Southern in the fall of 1965, Pepe would wait by the door for him to return. But he didn't get home often, and one day Durwood opened his campus mailbox. There was a letter from Ella Mae.

Pepe had died. "I do believe he grieved himself to death," Ella Mae wrote.

When he was teaching at Westminster, he inherited a dog from a relative who lived in Thomaston. He named the dog "Doots" in honor of his aunt. Her real name was Mary Kate but everybody called her Doots.

Doots, the dog, was a freak show right out of a Carson McCullers' story.

"She would have been a purebred German Shepherd," Durwood said. "But another dog got in and ruined the whole litter."

Durwood's close friend, Nancie McManus, herself a lover of animals, described Doots as having "the body of a German shepherd and the head of a manatee."

What Doots lacked in looks, she made up for in personality. She salivated like Pavlov's dog – not when she heard a bell but when she spotted the golden arches.

She loved McDonald's more than life itself. Forget the Gravy Train. Her ideal meal consisted of "two all-beef patties, special sauce, lettuce, cheese, pickles, and onions on a sesame seed bun."

In Doots' case, though, hold the lettuce.

"If I had her in the car with me, and we passed the McDonald's on Roswell Road, she would start whimpering," Durwood said. "She knew the sight of those golden arches. The night she was having her puppies on top of my dirty clothes in the laundry room, I was feeding her three Big Macs while she was popping them out."

After his friend Casey died, Durwood adopted two of his cats. Casey called one "Tarnation" because she was always into some kind of mischief. He found himself hollering "What in Tarnation?" so often the cat answered to it. Tarnation was born with a badly deformed right ear, and Durwood spent $1,200 at the veterinarian just to keep her alive.

Durwood and several of his friends found Kip when they were cleaning out Casey's house. Kip got his name because that's what Casey's family used to call him.

It took Simba a while to warm up to life with Durwood. He got his name from the character in "The Lion King."

"He would be dead in a minute if Casey and Jerry (Cooper) had not found him in south Atlanta and brought him to me," Durwood said. "He was eaten up with fleas and worms. He was raising himself in a part of town where people can't even feed themselves, much less an animal."

He went to a local animal shelter to see about getting a black cat. It was Oct. 31. He knew, of course, it was Halloween. What he didn't realize was that a Georgia state law prohibits black cats from being adopted from animal shelters on Halloween and the day before. Some people might use them for inappropriate purposes.

He returned the next day and claimed a male. He named him "Boy."

"Don't you want his sister?" the lady at the shelter asked. "They have never been separated."

Durwood is convinced it was a marketing ploy, but it doesn't matter. That's how "Girl" came into his life, too.

So the five cats now live with him. Or maybe it's the other way around.

They co-exist with a large, salt-water aquarium of tropical fish. The place is crawling with felines – on his computer keyboard and at the foot of his bed.

"Because I travel a lot, cats are so much easier than dogs," he said. "They're more independent. They can use the litter box. A dog would tear the place up."

A friend, Ann King, owns a company called "Blooming Cookies." She began the business in 1984 in her Atlanta home and delivered her products in a baby blue station wagon. It has now become a successful customized cookie and gift company.

Ann is also active in animal rights in the Atlanta area and was past-chairwoman of the DeKalb Humane Society. She once had Durwood speak at a reception she was giving for a state-wide organization for rescue animals.

"She introduced me as Bob Payne from Washington, and I had

on my White House badge," said Durwood. "They were honoring a gentleman that night, and they wanted me to make a few remarks as an icebreaker. I said a few words, and then I doubletalked. Then I said a few more words and doubletalked again.

"The gentleman was about 10 feet away from me, and he started getting concerned. He thought I was having a medical emergency, and that I was melting right in front of him. He was very much in his 'rescue' mindset."

The man took Durwood by the arm.

I think what Dr. Payne is trying to say is ...

After Durwood regained the floor, he spouted off some more doubletalk. Once again, he felt the man tugging at his sleeve

Thank you, Dr. Payne. I believe what he means is ...

There were a few looks of horror in the audience of 125 people. By now, most everyone in the room had figured out Durwood was a doubletalking imposter.

Everyone, that is, except for the guest of honor.

"Most of them were catching on to my nonsense, so I decided to let it run its course," Durwood said. "We made a big right turn at the end. I don't know if someone eventually told him or he figured it out on his own that he had been a tad premature."

Durwood didn't want to embarrass the man on a night he was being recognized for his contributions.

Later, Durwood would tell folks it had been a night of firsts.

"I've been doing this for 27 years, and this is the first time someone has tried to 'rescue' me," he said. "If you don't mind, I'm going to 'dog-ear' this one."

Durwood and Jevon Cooper, one of the young men he mentors.
(Photo courtesy of Rebecca Fordham Black.)

A rising tide floats all boats

The audience was young, but the message was time-honored. It fit like a ball comfortably pressed against the leather pocket of a broken-in baseball glove.

The words found their way into the ears of a group of students from Georgia State University at a ceremony for first-year students.

Durwood talked about hope, faith and gratitude. He stressed the nobility of leading a life that not only helps others, but also helps others help themselves.

There is no such thing as a self-made man, he told them. We did not get here by ourselves. We stand on the shoulders of others.

"I used to teach English, so I choose my words carefully," he said. "If you think you got this far on your own, you're delusional."

They laughed, of course, but the words had traction. Among the students in the auditorium was David Odom, the young man from Georgia Southern who had become his personal trainer. Durwood recognized him in front of the large group. David beamed. So did his parents.

In the wide circle that has become his remarkable journey, Durwood has been giving back in his own way. David became more than just the voice in his head ordering him to do 20 more sit-ups.

Durwood not only became David's mentor, but also a role model for others in David's life – his brother, Daniel, and a quartet of close friends: Billy Bonney, Jeff Peeke, Russell Pirkle and Nick Fusco.

Durwood has a name for the six young men. He calls them "The Posse."

"He is such a people person and enjoys surrounding himself with people," said David. "For the Posse, it's good to have someone like him from the outside. We are all in our early 20s, and he's 61, so he brings a different element to the group. He's an optimist, and he always gives us great advice. He knows the right thing to say because he's had all these life experiences. His best quality is that he can relate to anybody – from my 20-year-old brother to my 89-year-old grandmother."

Durwood began to hang out with the Posse about the same time he started watching a comedy on HBO called "Entourage" about a young actor and the friends he takes with him from Queens, N.Y., to Hollywood.

"In my own way, I've had a posse all my life," Durwood said. "When I was younger, I liked to hang out with older people. But, when I started teaching school, it was just the opposite. Being with a younger crowd gives me a wonderful perspective. I learn as much from them as they learn from me."

He does allow himself to preach. He wants them to see the wisdom that comes from moderation. He wants them to understand the value of friendship.

"Dale Carnegie puts it best: 'You can make more friends in two months by becoming interested in other people than you can in two years by trying to get other people interested in you,' " said Billy Bonney. "The reason we have become such good buddies with Durwood is because he takes an interest in us. He wants to know how work is going and how our families are doing. One of the most difficult things all of us have tried to do since meeting Durwood is putting others before ourselves. People don't understand how hard it is until they try it. Durwood puts others before himself every day because he genuinely cares."

Durwood often will allow himself to be spontaneous when he is with the Posse. One Friday afternoon in October 2008, David asked if he would like to ride with them to Statesboro to attend Saturday's Georgia Southern football game.

An hour later he found himself on the road to Statesboro. The next afternoon, he found himself in another one of those Forrest Gump moments.

He flashed his fake "White House Staff" badge to a guard at the gate. Suddenly he was on the sideline during the game.

It was there he ran into a longtime friend from Macon, Edgar Hatcher, the father of Georgia Southern head coach Chris Hatcher.

David and several of the others spotted Durwood on the field. *How did he get down there?* They shook their heads. Soon the whole fraternity was shouting "Durwood! Durwood! Durwood!" from the stands.

"As I saw my Posse of pals old and new, I was filled with the realization that we are indeed our own best friend or worst enemy," said Durwood. "It was reassuring to know that it continues to be true. Nobody is going to look after you better than you. But it sure helps to have a support system in place, just in case. Georgia Southern didn't win the game that day, but I didn't see any losers, either. As David says, 'It's all good.' "

Durwood also has become a mentor for other young people like Eddie Williams, D. J. Hurst and Jevon Cooper.

He met Eddie at the Publix grocery store in the neighborhood. Eddie was working there.

"He had this infectious smile, and he was from Liberia," Durwood said. "He was in his 20s, and so positive and optimistic about everything. That was the draw for me to befriend him. He has such a different view of the world. He doesn't have the preconceived notions that come from growing up in America. It was no accident that we met. God put him in my life and put me in his life."

Eddie came to the U.S. with his family in 1999. He has a young daughter to support, so Durwood has provided some extra work to help him with his finances. Eddie has become his personal assistant, running errands and helping with the housekeeping. He looks after the cats when Durwood is on the road. He is industrious, with a positive outlook that is contagious.

Durwood also made a generous financial contribution to help him purchase 700 pairs of athletic shoes to send back to Liberia. He got Eddie a truck to drive to South Carolina to pick up the shoes. Eddie packed them for shipping, and then drove to Savannah to send them on a ship to Africa.

Durwood met D. J. when he went to Verizon to take care of some business with his cell phone. D. J., who is African-American, worked at a car stereo shop next door. He noticed Durwood's Cadillac Escalade with the "pimp" wheels and teased him. "You don't fit the profile," he said, laughing. He also asked him if he had considered putting in a satellite television.

When Durwood discovered D. J.'s love of cars, a friendship was in the making. D. J. now handles Durwood's vehicles – the Escalade and the BMW convertible – and chauffeurs him to the airport when he travels.

Durwood met 15-year-old Jevon Cooper through Jevon's father, Jerry. Durwood met Jerry at a bakery one morning. Jevon was 8 years old.

"At the time I was the only white person he had ever known," Durwood said.

He would take Jevon to the movies or out for ice cream. He encouraged him in his schoolwork. He prayed for him at night.

Late in the summer of 2008, Jevon moved to El Paso, Texas, where his mother was transferred with the Army.

It was an emotional sendoff. Durwood bought Jevon a cell phone so they could stay in touch.

The day he left he called Durwood, who put him on the speakerphone. D. J. had come over, and the two of them could hear some of Jevon's friends making noise in the background. Jevon told them to be quiet.

"I'm talking to my grandpa," Jevon screamed at them.

Durwood didn't think too much of it until he looked over at D. J., who had tears welling in his eyes.

"You don't understand what he just said, Durwood, and it's not really your fault," D. J. said. "In the black community, a grandfather is a sign of reverence because so many fathers are not part of the lives of their children. So, when he tells his buddies he is talking to his Grandpa, that's the ultimate. That's huge."

Durwood and mentor D.J. Hurst strike a pose on the driver's side of the Cadillac Escalade. (Photo by Ed Grisamore.)

Mary Lou Whitlock was one of his mother's closest friends.
(Photo courtesy of Pearl Whitlock.)

Threads of life

They paid their last respects on a summer morning, before the sun had time to break through the clouds and turn up the heat.

Not that Mary Lou Whitlock would have minded the warmth of the summer day. She worked more than half her life in cotton mills, so she was used to wiping sweat from her brow.

She had been one of his mother's best friends. Ella Mae and Mary Lou used to shell peas together on the porch and catch up on the village gossip.

Her funeral, in the chapel of Hart's Mortuary, came one month after her 95th birthday. So it was more a celebration of her life than echoes of deep sorrow.

She had requested her favorite hymn, "Let Others See Jesus in You," be sung, and lots of Mary Lou stories were told. There was joy in the remembering.

In a sense, her passing marked the end of an era in the former mill village of Payne City. She was among the last of the former mill workers who still lived in the village, members of a generation who toiled and sacrificed to provide a better life for their children.

"She used to tell us she worked at that same spinning frame for 50 years, and she wasn't going to have her kids doing the same thing," said her son Carlton. "She wanted a better life for us."

It was the only life she knew, though. She was born on the road to Damascus in Baker County, one of 10 children in her family. She went to work in the mills when she was 12 years old. She was a textile worker in Albany, Thomaston and Forsyth before she planted her feet in Payne City in 1926. She spent 45 years in Payne Mill, from the start of the Depression in 1929 until her retirement in 1974.

Mary Lou raised chickens in the backyard and raised five children – J.T., Marvin, Carlton, Pearl and Thomas – inside the small, white house at the end of Brigham Street.

She bathed those children in a No. 2 washtub in front of the fireplace. She made them wash behind their ears, too. But every child in the village belonged to her.

"Mother whipped half the kids in the neighborhood," said Carlton. "She wore this big, plastic belt and would take it off if she needed to take it off. Every kid was her kid."

She didn't spare the rod. And she would slap most everybody across the chest with her hand. It was the special way she often expressed herself. It was her love tap.

She watched all four sons go off to war – J. T. and Marvin to Korea, then Carlton and Thomas to Vietnam. Her knees wore out the floors praying for their safe return.

Mary Lou was a den mother for the Cub Scouts and taught Sunday School at Bellevue Baptist Church, where she was a faithful member for 78 years. She also served two years on city council in tiny Payne City. After losing her re-election bid in 1984, she took it all in stride.

"I might have lost, but I sure am going to stay for the victory party," she said. "I'm going to get me a biscuit."

She had no pretenses, said her pastor, Neal Wall. "A straight shooter who told it like it was," he said. In his days as a young minister at Bellevue, he once tried to get Mary Lou to hurry and board the bus with the other senior adults on a return trip from Callaway Gardens.

"Young man, I've got a seat on that bus and it's not leaving until my seat is in it," she said.

Her mind was sharp, right up until the end, although the years in the mill took a toll on her hearing. She lived alone in the same house in the village. She stayed even after the neighborhood changed around her and almost nobody around could remember when the mill closed in 1988.

They all moved away or passed away, and Mary Lou Whitlock took a final piece of that fabric with her.

A year and a day after Mary Lou died, Durwood got a phone call.

Stevie Pope's obituary was in the Macon newspaper. They were the same age and in the same grade.

"He was my first best friend," said Durwood.

While Mary Lou's death marked the last of the mill workers who still lived in the village, Stevie's death hit even closer to home.

The sons and daughters were being confronted with their own mortality. Stevie had gone to the doctor in December to have his hip checked. It was then they found the melanoma. Eight months later, he was gone.

Durwood remembered his childhood friend with hair so red it looked like his head was on fire. He was kind-hearted and soft-spoken, thoughtful of others and with a built-in moral compass. He was always fair. He did the right thing.

They played a million games of kick-the-can.

Stevie called Durwood "Dursey." He was the only person ever to do that.

"He was one of the greatest gigglers in the world," said Durwood. "Stevie was cool before cool was cool. He was small in stature but big in character. All the guys in the village looked up to Stevie."

When Durwood fell at the playground and broke both his arms, it was Stevie who was assigned to help his friend at Bellevue Elementary. He had to carry his books to class and help with his lunch tray in the cafeteria.

He had to help him to the restroom, and even undo the belt to Durwood's pants.

"Now, how did I get stuck doing this job?" Stevie asked.

"Because," Durwood said, "you're from the village."

They buried him beneath the tall pines on a summer day so still nothing moved at all. At the funeral, old friends from the village came to pay their last respects. They hugged and comforted each other and wiped the sweat from the gray around their temples.

"Great to see you," they whispered softly. "Sorry it has to be for such a sad occasion."

Durwood called it another example of Payne City folks inventing the concept of "extended family." But before everyone left in search of an air conditioner, Durwood found Kevin, who was Stevie's youngest son.

Kevin was 18, tall and thin with freckles and flaming red hair.

"It was one of the most magical moments of my life," said Durwood. "I felt like I was with Stevie. He had just changed his name to Kevin. It was another one of God's winks, a glimpse."

"Did you know your father used to call me Dursey?" Durwood asked. "No one else did. Just Stevie. Would you do me a favor, Kevin? Would you stand over there and call for me?"

Kevin, not quite sure what to do or how to react, stepped back and called:

"Durrrrrrssssssseeeeeeeeeyyyyyyy!!!!!"

On the slope of that hill, a few miles from the village but much closer to heaven, Durwood imagined the face and voice of his friend.

"Stevie Pope will always have a special place in my memory of those days and that special time," he said. "The author of 'Peter Pan,' J. M. Barrie, said it best: 'God gave us memories so that we may have roses in December.'

"With that in mind, I look forward to one day playing another round of kick-the-can with Stevie. Thanks for the memories."

Stevie Pope, third from left on front row (with hands in pockets) was a fellow Cub
Scout and one of Durwood's best buddies growing up in the village.
(Photo courtesy of Jeannine Morrow.)

The late Marvin Jones and his wife, Christine, hold photograph of their son, Bobby, who was missing in action in Vietnam. (Photo courtesy of The Macon Telegraph.)

Every time a bell rings

Bobby Jones was two years older and a head shorter, but Durwood looked up to him.

"Everybody admired him," Durwood said. "He was smart. He was a leader. He exuded character. It was a privilege just to say you knew Bobby Jones."

At Lanier High School, the ROTC cadets would parade every Wednesday morning. John Anderson was the colonel. Bobby was one of two lieutenant colonels.

So it was not surprising to Durwood and the others when Bobby became a doctor, enlisted in the Air Force and went to Vietnam.

"He was willing to do his part to make sure we had our freedoms and to preserve our way of life," Durwood said.

Like others who once sat beside Durwood in social studies and ate lunch with him in the school cafeteria, he would never see Bobby again.

In October 1972, Marvin and Christine Jones drove Bobby to the airport in Atlanta. They snapped photographs as he boarded the airplane.

They hugged him one last time. "He's going to be OK," Marvin told his wife. Bobby went halfway around the world to Southeast Asia, where Wednesday was already Thursday and his family's mornings were his nights.

He swapped 15 degrees in latitude and 19 degrees in longitude for rice paddies and monsoons. He drank milk from bamboo stalks.

He never came home.

Bobby, an Air Force flight surgeon, had been a passenger on an

F-4 on its way to deliver medical supplies on a non-combat mission to Vietnam in 1972.

The plane was believed to have crashed on Bach Ma Mountain, about 20 miles north of Da Nang, with Bobby and the pilot on board.

His mother and sister always remained hopeful. They kept his photograph on the mantel. His military uniform was tucked away for safekeeping. At 5-foot-4, he had been too small to play most sports, so he took up golf, like the famous golfer with the same name. He carried those golf clubs with him to Southeast Asia.

There were scrapbooks and albums. Letters from Bobby. Letters to Bobby. They remembered him on his birthday, along with the day he was reported missing in action. And every day in between.

The personal belongings could never replace the person, though. For years the family kept looking for Bobby with every ounce of faith and energy within them.

Christine and her daughter, Jo Anne Shirley, struggled for closure as doors closed around them. They continued to fight their own battle for news and clues.

"Both the most frustrating and most rewarding time of my life," said Jo Anne.

Christine can never erase the morning of Nov. 28, 1972 from her memory. It was five days after Thanksgiving. A friend had come over to visit. They had planned to do some baking in the kitchen.

"When she came to the door, I couldn't talk. I just started crying," she said. "I had this feeling."

The premonition was the same strange feeling that once swept over her when Marvin was in the Battle of the Bulge during World War II, just a few months before Bobby was born in May 1945. It was the same battle that Durwood's father, Jack Fincher, had fought.

Her husband had returned home from that frozen battlefield. The chilly day when two military officers knocked on the door at their home on Adrian Place will only be frozen in sorrow.

A few days later, a Western Union telegram arrived: "...ALL SEARCH EFFORTS THUS FAR HAVE BEEN NEGATIVE. SEVERE WEATHER CONDITIONS HAVE HAMPERED

SEARCH OPERATIONS."

For years, Jones had been the only Macon serviceman still listed as missing in action from the Vietnam War and the only U.S. military physician still missing.

On July 22, 2008, two months after what would have been Bobby's 63rd birthday, Jo Anne received a call at her home in Dalton, where her husband, Rudy, is a physician. Rudy and Durwood were classmates at Lanier.

Her 91-year-old mother was at the house, baking brownies for the local National Guard.

The family was notified that the latest search team, led by a forensic anthropologist, had made a discovery at what was believed to be the crash site. A military identification card had been found. Military records verified it had been issued to Bobby.

"It's almost as if the Good Lord was saying to us: 'It's time you got an answer,' " said Jo Anne.

The news brought peace of mind and confirmed what the family had believed all along. Bobby likely died on impact in the plane crash. He probably did not suffer. He was not taken prisoner. He was not tortured.

Christine had moved from Macon to Dalton to be closer to her daughter and son-in-law. Her husband, Marvin, was a longtime educator and former assistant school superintendent in Bibb County. He died in 1994.

A memorial marker for Bobby is located next to his father's grave in Riverside Cemetery in Macon, not far from the I-75/I-16 interchange that now bears his name.

There is no official date of death on the headstone, just an inscription that reads: "Missing in Action South Vietnam November 29, 1972." It is followed with another inscription: "Presumed Killed in Action August 29, 1978."

At Andersonville National Cemetery, near the town where his mother grew up, there are rows of white markers stretching across the field. Among the 18,000 markers is one bearing Bobby's name.

At the time the family was informed Bobby was missing, Jo Anne was teaching fifth grade in an elementary school near Augusta, where Rudy was in medical school.

For the longest time, she convinced herself that her brother would be found, never dreaming her own search would stretch across pieces of four decades.

Nor could she have known she would become chairwoman of the National League of Families of American Prisoners and Missing in Southeast Asia, an organization dedicated to the 1,754 Americans still missing and unaccounted for in Vietnam. She also co-founded the Georgia Committee for POW/MIAs Inc.

What began as a crusade to learn what happened to her brother soon developed into a cause greater than herself. She became a champion for families seeking the same resolution she sought.

"She must have been a student of Churchill," said Durwood, "because she never gave up."

She never backed down from the challenges. She spent a fortune of her own money searching for answers. She made four independent trips to Southeast Asia to meet with government officials and lobbied countless elected officials in this country to make her voice heard.

In 1999, she received the prestigious George Washington Medal, a national award given annually since 1949 by the Freedoms Foundation at Valley Forge. Among the past recipients were actor John Wayne and Supreme Court Chief Justice Warren Burger.

She kept the issue of accountability alive. And, because of her efforts pushing through legislation, black flags with the POW/MIA emblem now fly at rest stops and weigh stations across Georgia.

While Jo Anne was on the front line, her mother worked behind the scenes, selling everything from handmade pins and artwork to writing her own cookbook, with proceeds going to the national POW/MIA organization. She once made tiny figurines of doves, each carrying the name of a POW/MIA from Georgia, to hang on the Christmas tree at the state capitol.

Christine and Marvin Jones were among the 36 families who were charter members of Riverside United Methodist in Macon. The church was holding revival services the week Bobby was reported missing, and the members prayed every night for his safe return.

Later, the church bell was dedicated in his memory. For years, Christine would hear that bell every Sunday morning.

A few weeks after the news came that would bring the Jones family the closure it had sought for so long, Durwood traveled to Dalton to visit with Jo Anne, Rudy and Christine.

Over a bowl of soup and a sandwich, he learned that the bell was no longer operating and was in need of repair.

He vowed to make sure the funding would be there so it would soon be ringing again.

Durwood was reminded of the final scene from one of his favorite movies, "It's a Wonderful Life."

Every time a bell rings, an angel gets his wings.

The I-75/I-16 interchange in Macon is named in honor of Maj. Bobby Jones. (Photo courtesy of Christine Jones.)

Durwood, posing as a roving reporter for BSTV, looks perplexed while interviewing people on the streets on Manhattan. (Photo courtesy of Durwood Fincher.)

Waiting to exhale

On a December day in 2007, Durwood sat in the Ronald Reagan Airport in Washington, D.C. waiting for a flight back to Atlanta.

Eight years earlier, he had been sitting in this same row of seats at the same gate when he got the call that his pastor, Frank Harrington, had died.

This time, he was the one making a call.

He dialed the number: 703-684-0555.

Four miles across town, skipping through the Virginia suburbs of Arlington to Alexandria, the operator answered.

"Washington Speakers Bureau."

He identified himself and asked to speak to Harry Rhoads Jr., the CEO and co-founder of the most prestigious speakers bureau in the world.

"Harry, is that offer still good?" Durwood asked.

"It was never off the table," said Harry.

Thus began yet another step in the journey.

The boy from the cotton mill was in high cotton.

Among the clients the Washington Speakers Bureau represents are Colin Powell, Tony Blair, Alan Greenspan, George Will, Tom Brokaw, Newt Gingrich, and Rudy Giuliani.

But it was much more than that. Durwood had actually been with the Washington Speakers Bureau since the 1980s. On this day he was becoming one of many prominent "exclusive" speakers at the bureau.

In a sense, he was being called up to the big leagues. Permanently. Since the offer had been extended years ago, he was calling himself up to the big leagues.

For years he remained connected with about a dozen other speakers bureaus out of loyalty. They had helped him get where he was going. And they were geographically positioned to give him the maximum exposure from groups looking for his brand of corporate comedy.

Now, Durwood was putting all his eggs in one basket.

"It was a godsend, a relief at this point in my life," he said. "It brought peace because the Washington Speakers Bureau handles everything for me.

"I was doing my own travel bookings and scheduling," Durwood said. "I was a one-man band. Everything had gotten so scattered, covered and smothered with the minutiae. I had stopped invoicing people. I was swamped with paperwork. I was trying to be all things to all people, and it had gotten completely out of control."

The Washington Speakers Bureau was founded in 1979 by Rhoads Bernie and Paula Swain. Durwood's first communication with them came not long after that – in the form of a rejection letter.

"I applied to become a member and got back the standard form letter," he said. "They were nice about it, but it was one of those: 'Don't call us, we'll call you' answers."

He finally got his foot in the door when Tony D'Amelio joined the Washington Speakers Bureau in 1984.

Tony and Durwood first met through an organization called the National Entertainment and Campus Activities Association (NECAA). It was a talent fair for colleges and companies looking for speakers, lecturers and musical entertainment.

Tony was an agent who was booking different acts and musical groups. He had gone to Atlanta for a showcase. Durwood was among the performers who were there, and it was difficult not to notice his unique act.

"He was wandering around and had all this energy," Tony said. "He was coming off the success of Toe Floss, and he had barrels of that stuff, which we all thought was pretty amazing. He caused quite a buzz."

Tony remembers sitting on the steps of the convention center that day with Tim Collins and Steve Barrasso, who went on to manage the rock band, Aerosmith.

"Durwood was with us, and he was feeling a bit mischievous. So he went down to the street corner where a cop was directing traffic and doubletalked him while asking for directions," Tony said. "I will never forget the look on that guy's face."

Tony found Durwood's act to be unique and intriguing.

"He was doing something different," he said. "There were some other people out there who were put-ons and imposters. But he was the only one I had come across who was also doing the doubletalk. What also made him appealing was, not only was he funny, he was a nice guy. He was likeable. He was fun to hang around with and what he did was never done in a mean-spirited way."

Tony later used his position and influence to bring Durwood on board with the Washington Speakers Bureau. He was not exclusive. He was just one of the hundreds of other speakers who were household names only in their own homes.

"I was very much an unknown, and they took a chance on me," Durwood said. "I knew if I screwed up, that would be the end of it. Their name would have been tarnished."

He began getting a lot of engagements through them and, in 1999, he was issued an invitation to go exclusive.

"It was at a time in my career when I was still with all these other bureaus, and these were the people who had helped me get started," he said. "I couldn't see cutting them off, so I turned it down. I was still with the Washington Speakers Bureau. Nothing had changed."

After nine years, though, the time had come.

"I was 60. I was trying to streamline my life. I needed to simplify," he said. "But I didn't know if the offer was still on the table. I was very nervous about making that call. There was an ocean of self-doubt. It's like why some people don't want to go to the doctor because they don't want to know what is wrong with them."

The decision brought him great peace. It also was a great day for Tony, Harry and others at the bureau. (The Washington Speakers Bureau still co-brokers with other bureaus and has a good working relationship in booking Durwood for events.)

"I've been trying to get Durwood under our roof for a long time," Tony said. "When you admire somebody, and you see them struggling to handle things that aren't in their nature, you want to help them. It was difficult for a right-brained person like Durwood to sit there and try to keep his schedule straight, negotiate for himself and return phone calls to all these different agencies. As a friend, I told him he needed to focus on what he did best. It wasn't going to cost him anything. All it was going to do was consolidate everything. He had finally had enough. It's one of the smartest decisions he ever made. He now actually has time to breathe."

A more relaxed Durwood is now "exclusive" with the Washington Speakers Bureau.
(Photo by Jake Saunders.)

Mr. Fincher takes a bite out of the Big Apple: Getting his nose powdered before going on the set of NBC's "The Today Show." (Photo by Jake Saunders.)

The Big Top

New York is the city that never sleeps. There is no darkness. When the sun goes down, they flip a switch in Manhattan and trillions of light bulbs take over.

On the night of May 22, 2008, Durwood looked out from his 31st floor window at the Marriott Marquis above Times Square. He could see the headlights of orange taxicabs. He could see the afterglow of the Broadway theatres and all-night diners.

He could not sleep in the city that never sleeps. He was tired, but he was very excited.

In the morning a limousine would pick him up at 7:30 and whisk him away to the famous studios of NBC. They would powder his nose and comb his hair, iron out any wrinkles in his slacks and have him wait in one of the most famous "green rooms" in the world.

He was going to be on "The Today Show" with Kathie Lee Gifford and Hoda Kotb.

At age 60 he was on the biggest stage of his life.

He had come a long way from the kitchen pantry back in the village, when Ella Mae would stop baking biscuits just long enough to take her seat in the one-woman audience.

There was another "stage" in his life that led him to this one. And he wasn't even on it. An improbable chain of events stretching back more than three decades had led him to this moment.

It started with going to see Gail Wilson in that one-act play back in Columbus in the early 1970s. It was Gail who later introduced him to her neighbor, Atlanta Braves pitcher John Smoltz.

Smoltz thought so highly of Durwood that he mentioned him

to former pro football great and sportscaster Frank Gifford when the two were playing together in a charity golf tournament. Smoltz gave Gifford one of Durwood's promotional DVDs.

Gifford, of course, was married to Kathie Lee, a former beauty queen who was a host with Regis Philbin on the popular talk show, "Live with Regis and Kathie Lee."

She was getting ready to leave the house one day as Frank was munching on some popcorn and watching the DVD of Durwood doubletalking the Braves players.

"Watch this," he said.

Kathie Lee mentioned "Mr. Doubletalk" to producer Michael Gelman, and the wheels soon went in motion.

That led to his first of 14 appearances on the show. Comedian Tom Arnold was co-hosting for Regis during Durwood's first appearance.

Kathie Lee, of course, was in on the joke. Appropriately enough, it was the April Fool's Day show. Durwood played the role of a doubletalking meteorologist, befuddling Arnold with talk about climate change and El Nino.

"After the show I didn't even have time to change clothes before they whisked me away in a limo," Durwood said. "When I got to the airport, a woman standing in line, two women on the plane and two of the flight attendants all recognized me."

Over the years he would do man-on-the-street interviews for the show on everything from 401K plans to marriage counseling on a Valentine's Day show. When Kathie Lee left the daytime talk show, Regis invited him back to doubletalk his unsuspecting new host, Kelly Ripa. The look on her face was priceless when he was brought in to play the role of a movie critic discussing the Academy Awards.

Fred Suss was a talent consultant who was instrumental in getting Durwood his first national television exposure. Fred had worked with the William Morris Agency. He became aware of Durwood while working with Production Group International (PGI).

He would book entertainment for corporate events, and had dealings with comedians such as Rita Rudner and Chris Rock.

"Durwood reminded me of Norm Crosby," Fred said. "He

would make up words and sounded like mish mash. I had seen his promotional tapes of the Braves and some of his corporate videos. He was very funny. But what impressed me when I met him was his genuineness. He was a great guy who cared about people. He was grateful for his success and counted his blessings. His comedy made people feel good."

Durwood's multiple appearances on Regis, one of the few live shows on television, also led to a working relationship with Kenny DiCamillo, an agent with the prestigious William Morris Agency.

Kenny represented both Regis and Kathie Lee, even after Kathie Lee left the program in July 2000 to pursue her singing career and spend more time with her family.

In April 2008, Kathie Lee began co-hosting the fourth hour of "The Today Show" with Hoda Kotb. Six weeks later, through Kenny's efforts, Durwood landed a spot on the May 23 show.

Only Kathie Lee, producer Angela LaGreca and a handful of production people were aware of Durwood's identity. It was Angela's idea to bring him in as Bob Payne, a 60-year-old college professor from Georgia Southern. He supposedly had been awarded a two-minute spot on the broadcast because he had won a promotional search for the show's "biggest fan."

It was the perfect setup. "The Today Show" had done a program on location at the Georgia Aquarium in Atlanta when it opened in November 2005. Angela told everyone they were bringing the "biggest fan" to New York as a corporate favor to Home Depot founder Bernie Marcus, who was the financial clout ($250 million) behind the aquarium. That set the hook.

On Thursday she sent a memo to Kathie Lee and Hoda. She said she had called Bob Payne on the phone and he was very excited and nervous about being on the show and meeting them.

"He sounds like quite the character," she wrote in the memo. "He has a bit of an accent and is very sweet. I've never been called ma'am so many times in my life."

An e-mail also was circulated that included a bogus feature story from Atlanta Daily World, dated April 13, 2008. There was also a memo called: "About Bob Payne – Today's Biggest Fan."

Bob is 60 years old and from Atlanta, Ga. He teaches English at Georgia Southern University. He has a local cable show called 'Bob's World' where he goes off on topics in the news. (He says some people have dubbed the show 'Payne in the Neck' which he loves, of course.)

Bob says he's been watching The Today Show for 50 years and never misses a day. He has been to the plaza several times and claims to own more Today Show memorabilia than anyone in the world. (He is going to open a 'Today Show Museum' in his basement.) He owns every copy possible of 'The Today Show' on video tape, and is the president of The Today Show fan club.

His interest in 'The Today Show' is clearly intense. I spoke with him before he caught a flight today, and the guy is like a walking Today Show encyclopedia – he should just come here as our researcher. Bob seems affable and charming and could barely contain his excitement at the booking. (He is very nervous, but I told him how friendly and warm you two both are and that it would feel as if he was in his living room.)

When I asked him if he has a family he didn't answer and seemed a bit uncomfortable, so I didn't press him. I guess The Today Show family is his 'family.' He does love teaching – English and speech – and obviously cares a lot about the 'youngsters' in his classes. Apparently he has tried to schedule his classes so he can teach later in the day so he can watch the show live. When he can't do that, he always has a trusty VCR in the 'record' position, and has thousands of Today Show tapes, plus mugs, T-shirts, figurines, buttons, hats, autographed pictures, clothing, etc., throughout his house.

I'm sure you'll make him feel welcome and appreciated.

The Thursday before the show, Durwood was taken on a "tour" of the NBC offices as his "reward" for being such a loyal fan. With a TV camera crew in tow, Durwood "interviewed" Today anchorman Matt Lauer, weatherman and feature reporter Al Roker, anchorwoman (and Dateline: NBC host) Ann Curry and anchorwoman Natalie Morales.

Durwood had at least one connection with Roker, the affable news personality. Roker is married to ABC News correspondent Deborah Roberts, who is from Perry, Ga., about 30 miles south of Macon.

As they moved from office to office, Durwood was at the top of his game. He slammed them with a barrage of doubletalk.

Angela would pull her colleagues to the side and give them a heads-up. She told them he had done some television work in Georgia, which gave him the legitimacy of holding the microphone.

By the time the sun came up Friday morning at the corner of Broadway and West 46th, Durwood was ready to doubletalk the day head on.

He wasn't knee-knocking, nail-biting nervous. After all, he had been on national television before. He had spent half his life in front of cameras and big crowds.

Still, there were a few butterflies when the limo driver pulled up at the back door at Rockefeller Center.

There was absolutely nothing that could stop him now.

Nothing, that is, except for maybe Ted Kennedy.

Three days earlier, Kennedy had been diagnosed with a malignant brain tumor. If something happened, Durwood was told he would be "bumped."

There were four people assigned to him in the makeup room. They had him take off his jacket and began working on his face.

"This guy came over with all these brushes to do my hair, and I told them I didn't want to look like a dead guy," said Durwood. "I told him I was supposed to look like an idiot."

"Well, then, you look fine to me," the makeup man said, laughing.

He could feel Ella Mae's presence with him every step of the way. He remembered what a friend had once said to him.

"I can imagine how proud your mama would be of you," she said.

And he told her: "It's like a relay race. She passed me the torch, and I want to keep it going."

He sent his pastor, Vic Pentz, a short note before he left for New York.

"I'm headed up north, and I hope to represent all of us well," he wrote. "There will be millions of people watching. My goal is to put in a little plug for our boss."

Vic sent him back an e-mail.

"I'll be watching for that," he said.

More than ready for the biggest stage of his life. (Photo by Jake Saunders.)

A hug from Kathie Lee Gifford brightened what was already one of the best days of his life. (Photo by Jake Saunders.)

Hoda Kotb, left, leans in and tries to make sense of what Durwood is saying on the segment of The Today Show on May 23, 2008. (Photo by Jake Saunders.)

Durwood gets one of those familiar baffled looks from news anchor Ann Curry of NBC. (Photo by Jake Saunders.)

It's good to laugh

A "green room" is the theatrical name for a room where actors and actresses wait before it is their turn on stage. It's the purgatory between the dressing room mirrors and the glare of the spotlights.

The origins of the word date back to the stages of 16th century London, when such rooms were most likely painted green to provide a soothing color for frazzled nerves and sweaty palms.

"I really don't know why they call it the Green Room," said Durwood. "I've been in a lot of them, and none of them have ever been green."

At about 10:30 a.m., Durwood was ushered to the set. Kathie Lee and Hoda were finishing up a heartwarming piece about a visually impaired young woman who was getting a makeover.

"You OK?" the floor manager asked as he checked Durwood's microphone and got him some water.

"Oh, yeah!" said Durwood. "I'm excited. I'm nervous, but it's a good nervous. I feel like a kid at Disney World. Dreams do come true."

A crowd of about 60 NBC employees was starting to gather off camera. Word had gotten out that a "joke" was going to be played on Hoda during the last segment of the show.

The floor manager told Durwood his name was Charlie. He knew about the doubletalk. He had seen the "interviews" from Thursday and thought they were terrific.

He said he had been with NBC for 34 years. When Durwood congratulated him for his loyalty to the company, Charlie told him working for NBC was like working for family. He said several of his co-workers also had more than 25 years with the network.

Minutes before the cue came to take Durwood onto the set, Charlie asked if there were any "last-minute instructions from Mr. Doubletalk."

"Charlie," Durwood said, "going along with what we were talking about family, I told a whole pile of people at my church back in Atlanta that I was going to give a little plug for our boss."

Charlie nodded. Durwood knew they were speaking the same language.

"What do you plan on doing?" Charlie asked.

"I don't know," Durwood said. "But it will be at the end, and it will be very unobtrusive. It's not going to be verbal. I'm not going to do anything crazy. But it's my goal to do something."

Charlie gave him the green light.

His segment was supposed to last only about two minutes. Although Angela was hopeful, she also was ready with the hook. After all, Durwood was an unknown quantity. She hoped he would be a smash hit. There was also a chance he could come across as the village idiot.

As the cameras focused on Durwood, a friend had taken an early lunch break to watch Mr. Doubletalk on "The Today Show." His buttons were popping. There were tears of pride in the corner of his eyes. He had confidence in Durwood. He remembered the old saying:

They laughed when I sat down at the piano.
But then I started to play …

KATHIE LEE: We're back with a very special guest. He's a man who claims to be Today's biggest fan.
HODA: Biggest.
KATHIE LEE: He says he's been watching … he's watched more hours of the Today show and owns more Today show memorabilia than anybody else. So in the spirit of feel-good Friday, we're making Bob Payne's dream come true, and we've invited him to come see where it all happens.
HODA: Hello, Bob!
DURWOOD: I'm telling you right now, I can't believe I'm here. It's

taken years. But I have to ask both of you one thing.

HODA: Yeah, go.

DURWOOD: (Unintelligible) ... I guess really with the broadcasting, which I've doing down in Atlanta a lot, and the Georgia Southern University where I'm a professor.

HODA: Uh-huh.

DURWOOD: I teach English and I ... (unintelligible). Has that occurred here? Has it?

KATHIE LEE: No. Unh-unh.

HODA: No.

DURWOOD: No? Well, I mean – I mean, the reason I ask you is several people have – well, nobody has really come up and asked me, but I think that a lot of times the question comes down to what, if any. And if not, how much?

KATHIE LEE: I've never – none for me.

HODA: No, none for me, either.

KATHIE LEE: But you've heard that a lot?

HODA: Mm-hmm.

DURWOOD: More than my fair share.

KATHIE LEE: Really?

DURWOOD: I really have been – I've been ... (unintelligible) ... to what we have, and I guess ... (unintelligible)... a gift.

KATHIE LEE: Times have changed so much.

HODA: Yeah.

DURWOOD: I don't mind change. I just don't want to be there when it happens.

HODA: Well, tell me – all right. Well, tell me – tell me about your house first of all, because we hear you have a lot of memorabilia, Today Show stuff. What kind of stuff do you have in there?

DURWOOD: Oh, you're talking to me?

HODA: Yeah.

DURWOOD: I'm sorry. I'm sorry. I told you.

KATHIE LEE: He's a little nervous.

DURWOOD: I told you. I may be in the business, but...

HODA: I'm only talking to you. That's the only person we're going to ... come here, give me a hug.

KATHIE LEE: Oh, no.

HODA: Ah, yes, yes, yes, yes!

DURWOOD: Thank you.

KATHIE LEE: Be careful. He told me before that he thinks you're exotic and gorgeous.

HODA: Excellent. Excellent.

DURWOOD: But let me just slow that down.

HODA: OK.

DURWOOD: When ... (unintelligible) ... really down in Atlanta ... and when I say Atlanta, of course, I mean Atlanta.

HODA: I've heard of that place.

DURWOOD: But coming up here to New York ...(unintelligible) ... I guess really one day I'm hoping of course that there will be people out there, but ...

HODA: There are!

KATHIE LEE: We were kicked off the plaza, this is what it's come down to.

DURWOOD: Were you all too loud again?

HODA: We're too loud.

KATHIE LEE: Yeah. That happened to you one time in Atlanta. Tell that story.

DURWOOD: I got kicked off. I mean, I wasn't even there and I got asked to leave. I'm sorry, I'm sorry. I'm just so nervous. Last night I dreamed I was awake, and then when I woke up, I was asleep.

HODA: Bob. What's going ... are we in the "Twilight Zone"?

DURWOOD: I am, but I came that way.

HODA: Bob. Bob, tell me, when did this whole love of this Today show start? I mean, what was it about the show that made you sort of fall in love?

DURWOOD: Well, we got a television.

HODA: Yeah?

DURWOOD: And that was in the '60s. And I was thinking that one of the things that I like to ... (unintelligible) ... and then I guess really to stretch that out. I mean, I could go on and on, but I think

I really have said more than I ... (unintelligible).

KATHIE LEE: All right.

HODA: Anyway.

KATHIE LEE: Hoda, I've got to let you in on something.

HODA: What?

KATHIE LEE: We've been having a little fun.

HODA: What?

KATHIE LEE: This is a dear friend of mine.

HODA: Oh, this is a joke?

KATHIE LEE: Durwood Fincher, better known as Mr. Doubletalk.

DURWOOD: And have I got something for you, because I know you've got beautiful feet. I got you some Toe Floss.

HODA: I did not know ... wait, I had no idea what you were talking about!

DURWOOD: Kathie Lee's crying again.

HODA: What is this, Toe Floss?

KATHIE LEE: Hoda ...

DURWOOD: It's whenever you stick your foot in your mouth. (Unintelligible)

KATHIE LEE: ... it's Toe Floss.

HODA: So this was all a bunch ... wait, I don't understand.

DURWOOD: (Unintelligible)

HODA: Tell me the truth. What just happened?

KATHIE LEE: All right. You're going to go – we've got to go to a tape. I want you – I don't want you to feel bad, OK?

DURWOOD: Hoda.

KATHIE LEE: Yes. Yes, this happened just recently.

(Beginning of Durwood's interviews from the day before.)

DURWOOD: You're my favorite.

AL ROKER: Thank you.

DURWOOD: I do want to say this.

ROKER: Well, I appreciate it.

DURWOOD: (Unintelligible)...I guess really has a notion for the future.

ROKER: Right.

DURWOOD: You are my favorite.

MATT LAUER: Oh, well, that's nice.

DURWOOD: I mean, I ... now, please don't tell ... I mean, you are my favorite.

DURWOOD: And I teach speech.

ROKER: Uh-huh.

DURWOOD: Well, then, you know, what we have ... and then I guess – did you find that to be true on your path?

ROKER: What? What part?

ANN CURRY: You know, when things are going on and things are falling apart...

DURWOOD: It's ... and you ... stress is that feeling you feel when you're afraid you're going to feel a feeling you'd rather not feel.

CURRY: ...and you ... exactly.

DURWOOD: And what we have, such as myself, and the honor accorded to that union what we have ... and I guess really, too, right?

NATALIE MORALES: Exactly.

DURWOOD: (Unintelligible) ... with everybody. And I guess, really, what I'm saying is does that sound like Al? I think so.

CURRY: Um.

DURWOOD: Or I'd say it's going to be too close to call.

CURRY: I still don't know what you're asking me.

ROKER: What part? No, no, I'm sorry.

DURWOOD: Are you talking to me?

ROKER: Yeah. No, I didn't understand the question.

DURWOOD: Did you ... (unintelligible) ... that may something that may haul that or not?

LAUER: Did I what? Did I what?

DURWOOD: I also teach speech. I speech ... I mean, I teach. And I love that you knew what we have I guess with everybody.

MORALES: Mm-hmm.

DURWOOD: Now, see, everybody.

MORALES: Mm-hmm.

DURWOOD: I mean, again, you know, a few, has it?

MORALES: You know, it's ...

DURWOOD: It's hard to call.

MORALES: Yeah, it's hard to call.

DURWOOD: I'm not sure I asked you the right question.

MORALES: Well, I'm not sure what you asked me, I'm sorry.

DURWOOD: It's OK.

ROKER: You start so that I know you're saying something real, and then it's ... (gibberish). It's very much like what happens in my brain.

DURWOOD: Do you understand now why you really are my mentor?

ROKER: I think so. I think so.

DURWOOD: I love him.

DURWOOD: Ann, have you ever heard of Mr. Doubletalk? He's been trying to meet you for years. You were fabulous. Do you feel that ... know that this has been a joke? I'm Mr. Doubletalk. We ... look at this. I mean, that was such a – think about what you just said yes to.

MORALES: I'm like, `What?'

DURWOOD: Do you feel better?

LAUER: I'm such a ... you know, when she ... Angela said to me, she goes, `He has a very tough accent.' I'm going, `That's the understatement of the freaking year.'

DURWOOD: No, no, no.

LAUER: I'm going, `This guy goes into – I don't – I don't know where it goes, it just goes anywhere.'

DURWOOD: I'm Durwood Fincher, Mr. Doubletalk. You were fabulous. We just were having some fun. Don't say a word.

ROKER: I won't.

(End of clip)

KATHIE LEE: Derbert ... I'm sorry, Durwood, I'm laughing so hard.

HODA: Oh, my God, that was so good.

KATHIE LEE: Oh, my gosh.

HODA: I didn't know ... can I be ... I didn't know what you were

talking about, I was just latching on to your little ...
KATHIE LEE: Well, I ...
DURWOOD: I probably should feel bad but, I mean, she is a dear friend of mine and she said, `Let's get Hoda.' And I said ... (unintelligible). And Angela was so wonderful.
KATHIE LEE: Oh, my gosh.
DURWOOD: It's good to laugh.
HODA: That was brilliant.
DURWOOD: It's good to laugh.
HODA: Brilliant, brilliant.
KATHIE LEE: It's great to laugh. Mr. Doubletalk.
HODA: Yes, love it.
KATHIE LEE: Durwood, thank you so much.

At the end of the segment, which lasted almost six minutes instead of the allotted two, Durwood smiled. He lifted his eyes and his right hand in a gesture toward heaven.

Thank you, God.

Thank you, Mama.

It was a private moment on the biggest stage of his life.

He looked over at Charlie, who was giving him a big thumbs up.

Afterward, the producer came over and hugged him.

"Did you know that for more than five minutes you were in control of NBC's timetable?" Angela asked him. "You were a novice. You had a lot of little powder kegs you had to jump, so we only gave you two minutes.

"You were sitting in that chair, and everybody here was on pins and needles. We didn't know where this was going. We don't make a practice of bringing in doubletalkers who don't make any sense. It was an unknown element, a huge risk. For those fleeting moments, your actions dictated to the NBC world whether we would cut for a commercial or extend your segment."

Millions of viewers had been watching during that time slot. (His segment received such a response that it was replayed on July 4.)

"The Today Show" is a national brand. It first aired in 1952, when

Durwood was five years old, and is the third-longest running TV series in history behind NBC's "Meet the Press" and the CBS Evening News.

"How does it feel, Mr. Graduate?" Kenny asked Durwood.

"What do you mean?" said Durwood.

"Well," Kenny said. "It was your graduation day."

He took a taxi to LaGuardia for his flight home that afternoon. But he was so high from the day's events he probably could have flown home without an airplane.

The next 24 hours were a whirlwind. People stopped him at the airport and told them they had seen him on the show. His cell phone seemed to ring every 30 seconds. His inbox filled with congratulatory e-mails.

He drove to Athens that Saturday to attend a wedding for the nephew of his longtime friend, Nancie McManus, at the First Presbyterian Church.

Durwood had been scheduled to provide the entertainment for members of the wedding party the day before. But he had to cancel after he received the invitation for "The Today Show." Instead, the wedding party watched him on TV during the brunch.

At the wedding Durwood didn't want to cause a commotion. He was physically, mentally and emotionally exhausted. He wanted to keep his presence low key.

"The church was packed, and I was just going to stand in the back," he said.

Nancie had other ideas.

"C'mon," she said. "Walk in with us!"

"But I'm not family," Durwood said.

"You are today," Nancie said.

They walked in slowly. Heads were turning. Durwood heard the whispers. It's ... the guy ... from "The Today Show!"

"I felt like I was getting way too much attention," Durwood said. "At the reception, people were coming up to me. It made Nancie so proud."

A few days later Durwood headed to St. George Island in Florida to spend a few days at the beach with some friends. He flew into Tallahassee, then rode down the coast.

St. George is a barrier island, four miles out in the Gulf of Mexico. It's a long, tall drink of water, some 28 miles long and two miles wide at its widest point. It stretches across a portion of the Florida panhandle sometimes known as the "Forgotten Coast." With its laid-back atmosphere, only a handful of restaurants and no tacky amusement arcades, it was the perfect place to get away for a few days and decompress.

In a span of five days he had gone from the skyscrapers of Manhattan to an island where building codes allow nothing more than three stories high. He had gone from the most densely populated piece of real estate in the country, with nearly 67,000 people per square mile, to a stretch of solitary beach.

One morning he got up early to watch the sun rise over the Gulf. He felt the warm sun on his skin, the salt air in his face, the sand between his toes.

He noticed a young girl and her father walking on the beach near where he was standing. The child walked up to a cluster of broken shells and picked up one off the sand. It was long and arched.

"Look, Daddy! Wings!!!" she said.

"No, dear, that's just a shell," said her father.

She looked at the shell again and shook her head.

"Wings!" she said, and ran off down the beach.

At dinner that night he dined on oysters at a nice restaurant at the edge of Apalachicola Bay. The waitress was a middle-aged woman named Jessie. He had behaved himself on the doubletalk, but once Jessie had gotten all the orders correct, he decided to have a little fun before dessert.

"Jessie," he said. "Do you mind if I call you Jessie?"

"No," she said.

"Well, Carol," he said. "Would you *puh-lee-filt-nuloos-dirv-somor* and *baro-zig-wop-shen-maudre*. Don't you think?"

Jessie looked like she had been caught in the wake of a fishing boat across the marshes.

"Uh, sure."

He had a little more fun before giving her his business card. He rarely boasts about his celebrity status, but he allowed himself a little braggadocio.

"I'm Mr. Doubletalk," he explained. "You might have seen me on 'The Today Show' last week."

Jessie shook her head. A serious look crossed her face.

"Well, when you go home tonight, turn on Channel 6," she said rather matter-of-factly. "I'm in the commercial for the Piggly Wiggly."

Durwood interviews "Uncle Sam," who was selling "talking" Hillary Clinton pens at the Democratic National Convention in Denver in August 2008. (Photo by Jake Saunders.)

Politics and the art of doubletalk

It was the week of the Democratic National Convention in the mile-high city of Denver, Colo.

Bill and Hillary Clinton had already given their speeches to the delegates, and the Democrats were waiting for Barack Obama to deliver his much-anticipated speech.

A man was standing in a park in downtown Denver. He was wearing an "Obama for President" T-shirt. He had a badge that said: "White House Staff" around his neck.

A woman walked past and noticed the outrageous contrast.

"Are you serious? Or are you just confused?" she asked.

"Yes, ma'am," he said.

The man, of course, was Durwood Fincher. The Great Imposter was hard at work again.

He was wearing the Obama T-shirt just for fun.

He bought the "White House Staff" badge for $9.95 at Dulles Airport in Washington. He had started wearing it for almost every occasion. (He found it to be a great way to get a good parking place or a table at a crowded restaurant.)

After his celebrated appearance on "The Today Show," Durwood had been in conversation with an agent in New York about the possibility of taking his doubletalk routine with NBC to the Summer Olympics in Beijing, China, and the Democratic and Republican conventions.

Durwood was less enthused about the Olympics. He had never been fond of international travel. Besides, the doubletalk probably would not be effective in an arena where so many different languages were being spoken.

But the political conventions intrigued him. What better place to doubletalk than around a bunch of politicians? He would be on their turf.

Even when NBC's interest waned, and then subsided, he went through with his own plans to attend the Democratic National Convention in Denver and the Republican National Convention in St. Paul, Minn.

He had attended national political conventions before, but never both in the same year.

"I did not go to make a political statement," he said. "I just wanted to document I was there, the same way people go to take pictures of Niagara Falls. This was going to be a portrait of me."

He took his own cameraman, Jake Saunders, from Orlando, Fla. They cruised the areas outside the convention halls. They perused the perimeter.

Sometimes the best show is the sideshow.

Durwood doubletalked security officers and super delegates in Denver. He gave equal doubletalking time to street vendors and college students in St. Paul.

Just call it the "Flairness Doctrine."

He found slices of life in great big melting pots. There was a guy in a rainbow-colored turban and a Hillary supporter in Denver decked out in red, white and blue and wearing a tall top hat.

He also did an impromptu show for the staff at the Marriott in Denver and made a 10-minute guest appearance on Neal Boortz's national radio show.

"The conventions surpassed all my expectations," he said. "I went fishing, and this is what I caught. I told people I wasn't with NBC or CNN but I had my own video guy with me. If nothing else, it would probably end up on YouTube. And that was good enough for them."

After he took two middle-aged women in St. Paul on his verbal bridge to nowhere, he asked one of them: "What was running through your head when I was *tureph-wuhl-bonup-sumor-herlost?*

"I was just thinking they didn't teach you how to speak down in Georgia," she said.

Durwood awards "Toe Floss" to a lucky vendor at the Democratic National Convention in Denver. (Photo by Jake Saunders.)

Man urges Durwood to "buy his book" at the Democratic National Convention in Denver. (Photo by Jake Saunders.)

Durwood back in the village: The man in the mirror smiled back.
(Photo by Ed Grisamore.)

Blue skies

The village still looks the same, but only if you have a good memory. The years have worn it and torn it, and its heart no longer beats as one. It's an empty pocket of its former self. There is no cotton mill to hold it together, like thread on a spool.

In the quiet of a Saturday morning, before most folks who live in Payne City had stirred, a man in a silver BMW convertible slipped down the streets.

As he slowed to a stop, a dog barked at him, as if he were an intruder. The dog must not have recognized the famous native son.

The top to the convertible was down, but he could not blame the tears rolling down his cheeks on the wind against his face.

He would not apologize for the puddles in his eyes, the tears of joy and sadness flowing like spigots.

These were tears for the ghosts of village past. These were tears for Ella Mae, Roy, Jack, Mary Lou and Stevie. These were tears dedicated to every soul who ever crossed the threshold of every home and became fellow pilgrims on his journey. These were tears for every game of kick-the-can, the footsteps of children running through the alleys, catching their breath as they hid under the porches in the dark.

The night before, Durwood had been to the theater with friends to see a musical based on the colorful characters created by Dr. Seuss. Theodor Seuss Geisel also made a living out of putting together long, strange words that made no sense.

But some of those words were full of wisdom.

"Don't cry because it's over," said the late, great Seuss. "Smile because it happened."

A few hours later, Durwood found himself in a room with more than 150 others from the village.

They come back every October, like homing pigeons, for the Payne City reunion. They don't need a compass to find their way.

Before the last drumstick was gnawed to the bone and they ran out of banana pudding back in the kitchen, Durwood stood to address the crowd. They were holding their heads high. Always have.

The year before, he had told them a book was being written about his life. Now, he was there to tell them it was finished. That wild and wonderful collection of scattered stories had been captured and tamed. Those people and places had been brought back to life and pressed between the pages.

He showed them the cover of the book and then told the story behind the title – thank you, Grandpa Fincher. They laughed until their sides hurt.

Yep, if anyone was going to be in the circus, it was Durwood.

And then he said something that touched them. He said it was as much their story as it was his own. A man is the sum of his parts.

They all knew his Mama. He had dedicated the book to her. It was Ella Mae who gave him roots, then wings.

Yet he took something from every one of them. Pass the turkey and dressing. He was at the table for Thanksgiving.

He told them about riding through the village that morning. The flesh and blood of the village was gone, and only the skeleton had been left behind.

But he was not dispirited.

In his mind's eye he could still see the auditorium, even though it had been torn down 26 years earlier. It was his first stage.

Along his memory lanes he could still hear the sound of the mill whistle.

The tears started up again.

"This book is a testament to you," he said.

There were so many hugs and handshakes as he headed out the door, he had to hurry to make it to the airport for his flight later that afternoon.

By sundown his wheels would be touching down in Las Vegas, which is a long way from Booger Bottom.

But before he left Payne City, he drove through the village one more time.

On a narrow street behind Comer Terrace someone had left a large mirror propped against a fence. It was there with some other trash to be picked up.

He pulled his car even with the mirror, looked across at eye level and saw his reflection.

He smiled.

The man in the mirror smiled back.

Then Durwood Fincher, a man in love with life and at peace with his past, drove away.

There was nothing but blue skies ahead.

"Do not be afraid to show your emotions." (Photo by Maryann Bates.)

Do what?

Durwood Fincher's "To Do" List

- Do unto others as you would have them do unto you.
- Do the right thing.
- Do not block a blessing.
- Do have a belief system.
- Do not forget your roots.
- Do not feel sorry for yourself. Ever.
- Do not forget to call home.
- Do believe in magic.
- Do not forget the stray and unwanted animals of the world.
- Do not underestimate the power of a hug.
- Do understand the value of an encouraging word.
- Do not forget the "invisible people."
- Do not be afraid to show your emotions.
- Do remember when you begin to give you begin to live.
- Do not be ashamed to say the blessing in a restaurant.
- Do learn to see God in everything.
- Do what you know.
- Do it often.
- Do it for free.
- Do look before you leap. … But leap.
- Do care.
- Do not take it all so seriously. It's just money, and most of it's not even yours.
- Do look both ways. It's still true.

"I do believe you're having a Toe Floss moment." (Photo by Maryann Bates.)

Doubletalk glossary

Agaplavess-maleda-wudockasha --- I believe you're having a Toe Floss moment.

Barock-obahma-foor-prez – America is the greatest country in the world. Help me change it.

Deewsov-laralech-sworos-tomoth – Bless her heart.

Formowormora-tomentay-falloopa-commisso – Nobody is completely worthless. You can always serve as a bad example.

Harbery-alberder-gotsteppen-lichaswish (Catholic version) – Everybody is somebody's pope.

Jumishil-notchamo-sackemahre-wofertom – (Mr. Bubble's version) – Everybody is somebody's soap-on-a-rope.

Lapetorut-buddegrandon-rossmonsnap – Life is just a tire swing.

Muhrreee-homperhon-imaguhlesh – We might need to do a background check on him.

Nastyerhan-yellosub-pennylayne-hayjude – Paul is dead. Paul is dead. Paul is dead.

Pawritzing-minisual-eorgen-nacomag – I'll have fries with that.

Slivren-pockenot-koobheten-warebe – The rain in Spain falls mainly on the plain.

WaWamon-digosh-skulis-prefonda – Do what?

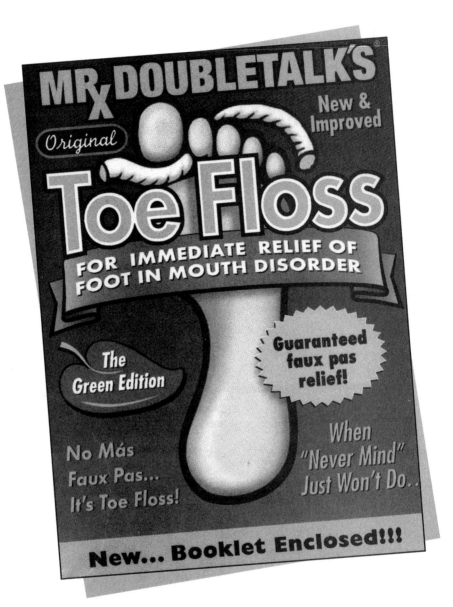

For additional copies, booking information,
Toss Floss orders and to read Durwood's blog,
please visit www.doubletalk.com